CAREVISION

**THE WHY AND HOW OF
CHRISTIAN CAREGIVING**

JERRY K. ROBBINS

CAREVISION

THE WHY AND HOW OF
CHRISTIAN CAREGIVING

Valley Forge® Judson Press

Carevision: The Why and How of Christian Caregiving

©1993

Judson Press, Valley Forge, PA 19482-0851

Printed in the U.S.A.

Bible quotations in this volume are from NEW REVISED STANDARD VERSION of the Bible, copyrighted 1989 by the Division of Christian Education of the National Council of the Churches of Christ in the United States of America, and are used by permission. All rights reserved.

Text of "A Mighty Fortress Is Our God" (chapter 5, note 5) copyright © 1978 LUTHERAN BOOK OF WORSHIP. Reprinted by permission of Augsburg Fortress.

Quotation (chapter 12, note 5) reprinted from CHRISTIAN CAREGIVING by Kenneth Haugk, copyright © 1984 Augsburg Publishing House. Used by permission of Augsburg Fortress.

Printed in the U.S.A.

Library of Congress Cataloging-in-Publication Data
Robbins, Jerry K., 1935-
    Carevision : the why and how of Christian caregiving / by Jerry K. Robbins.
        p.   cm.
    Includes bibliographical references.
    ISBN 0-8170-1195-1
    1. Caring—Religious aspects—Christianity. 2. Caregivers—
Religious life.
    3. Medical personnel—Religious life. 4. Theodicy. 5. Suffering—Religious aspects—
Christianity. 6. Pastoral psychology. I. Title.
BV4509.5.R622 1993
253—dc20   93-23840

To

Alice, Mark, and Paul,

Caregivers in their life and work

Two are better than one . . . For if they fall, one will lift up the other; but woe to the one who is alone and falls and does not have another to help.

Ecclesiastes 4:9-10

Contents

Preface

A person in a health profession recently said to me, "I know that what I am doing helps people. I just don't know if it makes any difference." What happens when caregivers begin to doubt that their work has any meaning beyond the immediate service it provides? Are you a care provider who wonders what it all adds up to? Perhaps you know a care provider who is at risk of burnout because of frustrations like these.

This book has been written for the purpose of assuring caregivers that their labors of love are important far beyond their direct curative or palliative effect. In the larger picture, often we do not know the good that results from what we do. Yet action alleviating suffering, when done with a spiritual component, makes a statement about pain, suffering, God, justice, and ultimate goodness in life that is far more effective than any rational arguments meant to solve the problem of evil.

Care providers are in a position to make a significant statement about suffering and what God is doing about it. They have a resource at their hands that can revolutionize the way we approach the problem of evil. That resource is *carevision*. Carevision is a style of helping that includes both insight and action. It is care offered with a spiritual vision, and it is envisioning the problem of evil as a problem to be managed with action. This book will help the care provider appreciate the profound implications of such intentional caregiving.

Whatever assistance you provide—as pastor, nurse, physician, social worker, volunteer aide, crisis interventionist, nursing home attendant, therapist, counselor, friend, or primary family support person—your work is extremely important. It is the kind of love-indeed that speaks far more forcefully than any words of explanation we can offer to those who suffer. Armed with carevision, you are a presence that is both physically and spiritually therapeutic. Your care means nothing less than a cogent, convincing, and coherent answer to one of the most persistent and pesky religious problems human beings face, the problem of evil.

PART ONE

The Need for Carevision

CHAPTER ONE

Getting our Bearings

Carevision saved my life. A few years ago, for a variety of reasons, including a mitral valve prolapse, my heart would not maintain regular rhythm. This disorder caused discomfort in my chest, fatigue, and bouts of depression. Through several cardioversions (a medical procedure in which a measured electrical shock is administered to the heart) and drug therapy, normal rhythm was reestablished and is being maintained. Though a relatively mild malady compared to what others suffer, it was for me a terrifying and revealing experience. Never again could I look at the problem of suffering as a mere spectator.

The physician who treated me was a Christian, as were many of the people who served my emotional and spiritual needs at the time. I am not prone to overdramatize situations, but I believe that had it not been for their compassionate efforts, especially in encouraging me to seek cardioversion, I would not be alive today. What all those people had in common was a commitment to deal with human suffering by trying to alleviate it. They had a *vision* that caregiving can be spiritually therapeutic. They did not debate about the problem of evil or try to explain why I had a heart malady. They simply tackled the physical problem and my mental distress with aggressive, corrective therapy. They offered *care* that was spiritually inspired by a goal of restoring health and wholeness. They were concerned helpers filled with the passion of carevision.

Carevision is just the opposite of the typical efforts to explain evil away through rationalizations called "theodicies." Unfortunately, none of these explanations of the problem of suffering are very helpful to those who suffer. When I was sick, theodicies were hollow comfort. What helped the most were all the procedures, therapies, and words of encouragement that led to my recovery—the carevision that informed and stylized the work of the caregivers around me. Thus carevision is both the *insight* that deals with the problem of evil by providing effective treatment to sufferers, and the *action* of giving care that functionally affects the sufferer. Carevision is an approach that combines care and vision: it is *care* offered with a spiritual vision, and it is a *vision* of evil as a problem requiring action.

Caregiver Burnout

If you are a professional caregiver, carevision could save your professional life just as it saved my physical life. It is the kind of resource that, if adopted as a personal philosophy, could bring new insight and energy to all care-providing vocations. My wife, an oncology nurse, regularly attends workshops and conferences intended to support and empower those who work daily in often critical life-and-death situations. These gatherings are invariably in pleasant therapeutic settings near the ocean or some large resort area. "Why do you get to go to such nice places?" I ask her. "Because we *deserve* it," she replies.

There would be no need for such exotic recuperation and refreshment if the work of caregiving were not so difficult. But clearly, many caregivers are highly distressed by their work. The caring professions are not exempt from the high burnout rate that afflicts many occupations. In response to this crisis, literature abounds on the importance of taking care of the caregiver, healing the healer, serving the servant.

What are the reasons for this burnout and malaise? Of course, many ingredients play into the stress in caregiving occupations: long hours on the job, dealing with institutional inertia, tensions in collegial relationships, repeated encounters with death, a sense of help-lessness in one's work, unfulfilled idealism. However, the most fundamental source of dismay threaded through this whole dark tapestry are those questions that are theological and religious in nature.

When our son was in medical school, he wrote a letter to us that included these lines: "Today we are slicing brains in anatomy lab. I have not found God in any of the sections, but I still look." Care providers who work on the edges of life and death confront a world of mystery and finality, where the question of meaning arises daily. A woman with a progressive disease entered my office after a recent medical examination and told me, "The doctor says I have another tumor and it is on my remaining good eye." Then collapsing in tears, she sobbed, "I don't know what's wrong with my life. What am I doing to make this happen?" Caregivers are never far from questions like these. Human beings are meaning-making creatures, and life at the edges threatens the center. Cohesion and purpose un-ravel under the relentless presence of suffering.

Part of the reason for the high level of stress in care-providing occupations is the persistence of this issue of meaning. Increasingly, care providers are being called upon to answer questions of deep philosophical and theological import. Along with the question of my friend, "What am *I* doing to bring about this suffering?" people regularly ask, "What is *God* doing to bring about this suffering?"

Sickness seldom visits us without bringing a companion, namely, spiritual perplexity. Harry Cole writes: "Every critical encounter in life is a matter of ultimate concern." Out of the experience of taking care of his sick wife, he describes the grappling of the caregiver: "You want to have faith that the illness has some ultimate purpose which you hope will become clear to you over time and in the course of your duties as a caregiver."[1] Suffering pushes us to plumb the murky depths of theology for an answer to why this suffering has to be. It thrusts us into the very face of God where we search for a reason for our distress. Christy Brown, who suffered a terrible de-bilitating illness, cried out in his anguish, " 'What was I,' I asked myself as I sat there? 'Just one of God's practical jokes!' "[2] Often caregivers find themselves in the middle of this religious dissonance and unrest.

Questions bombard the care provider from every angle. They often arise from those who receive care. Whereas in the past, counselors or clergy were the usual targets for these theological probes, today doctors, nurses, social workers, and even visitors are likely to be put on the spot. A professor of internal medicine wrote, "Once a dread diagnosis is made, the response almost inevitably begins 'Why me?' followed quickly by 'It isn't fair!' This requires activation of a personal theodicy."[3] Given this sequence, caregivers are likely to find themselves in a situation of playing resident theologian to those they tend. A medical student confided in me, "It is not the medical care that is so hard. It is when I allow myself to stand back a moment and look at my patients, really look into their eyes, where I see the real depth of their suffering—that is what bothers me." Whether willing or not, caregivers are often placed in a priestly role that demands the formulation of answers and the administration of spiritual counsel above and beyond mere maintenance care.

Questions can also arise out of the situation of the caregiver, from the stress of the circumstances in which care is offered. Some situations place tremendous burdens on those who supply the care, especially in the case of extended, progressive illnesses that impose uninterrupted and increasing demands on the caregiver. So pervasive is this problem that a special scale has been invented, the "Caregiver Burden Scale." By this scale, the amount of stress in a particular caregiving situation can be documented. Family care providers of dementia patients, for example, face such serious problems as social isolation, career disruption, time constraint, financial burden, and hard physical labor. Some of these care providers find that their role severely tests their religious faith. Angry with God, one asked, "Why me? I've been good, honest. How come? Can you—can anyone—answer that?—something basic is wrong."[4] The pressure of caregiving that is constant and consuming can push the care provider over the edge of an abyss of unanswered questions. Along with all the other tasks, the coping assignment now includes finding some resolution to profound theological problems.

A third level of questions can arise when the caregiver becomes the patient. Sickness or failure or crisis can also afflict the caregiver; indeed, typically we simply rotate in and out of roles as care provider and care receiver. When those who provide care find themselves in need of care— when caregivers become patients—theological probing takes on an intensely personal edge. Even those who are not particularly spiritual may find themselves wondering about things in new ways. In searching for the reason for his cancer, Fitzhugh Mullan, a young physician, asked, "Was I a victim of the supernatural—some malevolent and vindictive force disseminated by chain letter? . . . What act of hubris had I been guilty of? . . . What had I done wrong?"[5]

Mullan had been raised as a believer but functionally was neither religiously active nor inclined to faith, and his illness forced him into profound theological unrest. How much more is the perplexity of those vast numbers of caregivers with active religious faith who find themselves laid low by suffering? When such misfortune occurs, caregivers, like many other sufferers, are cast into the arena of theological warfare where survival depends on clear thinking, some useful religious resources, and a little help from friends.

Carevision: Action as a Resource

Where can people who provide care turn for assistance in dealing with the theological stresses associated with their work? Typically there are two types of resources available to caregivers who want to broaden and deepen their skills. On the one hand, there are manuals written by technicians that outline practical strategies for coping with suffering. Bookstores are filled with these do-it-yourself therapies for coping with cancer, beating depression, recovering from divorce, dealing with grief (an all-time bestseller), developing a prayer life, raising a teenager (!), and caring for elderly parents. In this age of take-control management, there is no end to the fix-it advice for those who have broken down in one way or another.

The other type of resource for suffering people is more cerebral. It is designed by religious writers and philosophers for those who are spiritually or mentally distressed by their suffering. Typical of these resources are such titles as *Holy Power, Human Pain* and *Is God Still Here?*[6] These texts deal with the abstract, theoretical questions of the source and meaning of suffering through the development of theodicies, or theological arguments to defend God by justifying evil in the world. These resources are enormously popular today, comprising a large part of the religious book market. An amazingly popular book of recent times is *When Bad Things Happen to Good People* by Harold Kushner.[7] This book became a publishing phenomenon throughout the religious and secular reading community, a fact that suggests the great importance of its subject matter. As well as wanting to *do* something about their plight, those who suffer want to know what to *think* about their unfortunate situation in life.

What is usually not available to stressed caregivers is a resource that incorporates the practical approach to suffering with the theological. A reader seldom finds the suggestion that what we do about suffering may have something to do with how we think about it. Efforts to explain the experience of evil and justify the ways of God are usually set apart from advice on what to do about it: they even occupy different shelves in the bookstore and different stacks in the library. There is seldom any reference to the practical as a resource for the theoretical. Theologians spin elaborate theories to soothe the troubled mind, and practitioners write manuals to reduce the level of suffering, and the two never meet. But surely this is to divide two areas or concerns that ought to be held together.

In religion in general, theory and practice are not to be separated. The Christian life especially is a life that confesses faith in God and acts in obedience to that confession. Jesus spent a great deal of his ministry dispensing information about the loving ways of the Father who is in heaven (Luke 15:11-32), and about reconciliation with that Father through the Son (John 14). Those are matters of faith, or theory-of-life issues, if you will. He also called people to a life active in love toward God and each other (Matt. 22:37-40). The Christian life is a matter of action or practice. Both constitute the Christian message. When people asked what they should do to be saved, Jesus answered that they should *believe* in him (John 6:28-29); to the lawyer who desired eternal life, Jesus advised active *caregiving* (Luke 10:25-37). The early Christians understood their Lord as one who both taught and acted (Acts 1:1), and their discipleship as involving both faith and action (Gal. 5:6).

Keeping faith and action together is especially important with the problem of suffering. It has been said that when lost at sea amidst dark skies and rolling waves, the best way to regain equilibrium is to go inside the cabin and fix one's sight on two points that are stable relative to each other. Intense, unrelenting suffering can cause us to lose all spiritual balance. The world becomes a nauseating blur, where the horizon disappears and all meaning falls out from under our feet. Caught in a vortex of pain, isolation, and despair, we can no longer find our way ahead.

At that point it becomes crucial to focus our concentration on the two certainties of the Christian way, belief and behavior. Faith and action are "fixed" relative to each other in the battle against suffering. To deny either is to forfeit a chance of making headway in wrestling with the awful problem of evil. We need to find both an effective way of coping with suffering and answers to the theological issues generated by suffering. More profoundly, in searching for a theological response, we need to consider the value of the practical coping strategies for addressing the theological issues. That is the particular concern of this book: namely, to suggest that in the very action of reducing suffering, something important is said about the Christian response to evil. I call that special strategy *carevision*.

Carevision is the antidote to a bifurcated treatment of the problem of suffering. Carevision is the ingredient that stabilizes the Christian stance in the face of evil. When confronting suffering, it is easier to use coping strategies alone or to write long treatises justifying the existence of suffering. But both of those efforts, when done in isolation, are insufficient. An even-handed management of suffering requires carevision. Carevision is both a call to action and a statement about God, evil, and the world. Indeed, in its counsel to do something about suffering it also offers a consideration for those troubled by the intellectual problem.

Carevision is *care* with an understanding of what that care can mean for those troubled in soul and spirit. It is a *vision* of the world reclaimed and redeemed by a God whose will is the healing of creation and whose plan is to enlist us in that transformation. Anyone who takes the approach of carevision will find a resource that can keep the ship of faith afloat through the awful storms of doubt and bitterness, perplexity and despondency that often darken the sea of suffering.

Preview and Promise

In this opening chapter we have located some of the benchmarks of this study and suggested the course we will take. It is now time quickly to survey the ground we hope to cover. In the next two chapters, we will complete Part 1 with a closer look at the failure of three common attempts to solve the problem of evil with words and some considerations in favor of an activist approach to the problem.

In Part 2 we will turn to the testimony of Scripture and tradition as a foundation for carevision. We will discover how the Bible does not so much argue about the existence of evil as tell stories of divine action overcoming evil. In exploring texts about the mighty acts of God (chap. 4), the campaign of Jesus against the devil (chap. 5), the miraculous cures wrought by Jesus (chap. 6), and the stories of resurrection from the dead (chap. 7), we will also examine several of the perplexing issues raised by the presence of evil.

Also important in the formation of carevision is a commitment to act for the alleviation of suffering. Part 3 examines some of the incentives for human caregiving provided both in the notion of vocation (chap. 8) and the call to Christian discipleship (chap. 9), and several of the areas where caregiving can be put into practice (chap. 10).

Finally, in Part 4, we will see just what kind of statements such actions make about God, suffering, and the order of things. We will consider three statements of carevision in action: God is our companion in suffering, not the cause of it (chap. 11); love, rather than evil, is the last word (chap. 12); and, suffering is an inevitable part of God's gift of autonomy to us (chap. 13). A concluding chapter will encourage the reader to develop the activist part of carevision.

What can the reader expect from this book? First, you will find support in the struggle to make sense of a world where God and human suffering go hand in hand. Jesus said, "Blessed are those who mourn" (Matt. 5:4). This book is for those who mourn over the brokenness of the earth, the human community, and the individual spirit, who anguish over the suffering inflicted on the human soul. You are not alone in your mourning.

Second, this book is a guide for finding your way through the vast literature of argumentation on the intellectual problem of evil. As no one can suffer for us, so no one can solve the problem of suffering for us. It is an intensely personal problem that must be solved by each person in his or her own way. Yet we can find help in seeing how others have struggled and survived. This primer provides at least an overview of the landscape on which the battle is fought.

Finally, this book is a manual on how to cope with turmoil in religious faith. It is not a manual for dealing with pain, hospital routine, disability, and all the myriad immediate aspects of human suffering, nor does it offer practical advice about regular physical maintenance under stress. But it is a manual with practical counsel for the equally weighty matter of faith in distress. It will help you cope with thoughts, feelings, and attitudes you may have about God's role in suffering.

As its author, I bring to this book periodic academic pursuit of the topic, years of reading about and ministering to those who suffer, and my own experience of sickness. The real voices in these pages, however, are the dozens of people I have had the privilege to know and be with through soul-wrenching illness and tragedy. Their courage and perseverance in faith is the source of light that illuminates these pages. Without that strength of spirit there would be little sunshine in so serious and solemn a project as this.

CHAPTER TWO

The Trouble with Words

"I just couldn't think of anything to say," the student anguished as he recalled a recent visit with a classmate who had just been diagnosed with leukemia. "I mean, we joked around like always, and I told him about what was happening on campus. But I couldn't get serious with him. There were times when he lay there staring at the ceiling saying nothing. I know he was thinking about his bleak prognosis. We had talked about other students whose lives were snuffed out in automobile accidents. I suspect he was also thinking about how lucky I was to be healthy. Yet I couldn't think of anything to say that would not sound phony or presumptuous. Words seemed so cheap at that time."

Carevision is an alternative to the embarrassment of hollow words. A common approach when facing the problem of evil is to offer rational explanations for the existence of suffering. However, too often these theodicies, designed primarily for intellectual relief in trying to exonerate God for the existence of evil, do not deliver what they promise. They are empty accounts in the storehouse of those who suffer, cheap consolations with no real substance. Those burdened with pain or failure, distress or despondency are little served by the words of well-meaning comforters. A case in point is the story of Job. Job was hardly buoyed by the "consolations" of his visitors. Indeed, he was cast into deeper and deeper despair the more they counseled him. It seems they provided the greatest support during the initial seven days, when they sat with Job in silence.

Carevision is a form of the familiar adage, "Actions speak more loudly than words." In the matter of dealing with the problem of evil, actions that alleviate suffering often say more than the words we offer for comfort. This is not to suggest that words have no place in dealing with the problem of evil. There is an important role for theology and the stories of faith in the management of suffering, as we will shortly see. However, it can be very difficult to come up with just the right word of faith, grounded in God's action and braced with realistic hope. We tend to work out a rational explanation that is more logical than faithful. Typically, these explanations qualify the power of God, qualify the goodness of God, or turn bad into good. They are the most popular words offered in a variety of forms to the afflicted. Let us see why they are more troubling than therapeutic.

Words That Enfeeble God

One sickbed strategy currently making the rounds goes something like this. There is a lot of suffering in the world that we should recognize and face up to. We should let each other know that we are in this problem together. We should also avoid efforts to justify evil or any theoretical solutions that weaken our resolve to fight against evil. But be assured, so the argument goes, that God is not the cause of this suffering. Rather, God stands with us in our suffering to help us. God is not to blame for suffering because God doesn't have the power to control or arrange the world. Bad things just happen. The rule that makes order possible also makes suffering possible. The fact is, we don't really know why there is suffering. But we can control what it does to us, and we can wrest some good from it. We can also recognize that this is the better arrangement because it allows us freedom. We should not pray to God for a miracle to end suffering, but for the strength and resolve to do something about it ourselves. In turn, God helps us through the work of physicians, counselors, and caring friends.[1]

While this approach may try to avoid rationalizing the problem of suffering away, it often includes efforts to justify God. Arguing that God doesn't have power enough to be blameworthy is simply a rationalization. So is the companion maneuver that says, after all, the world is better if God isn't all-powerful because then we can enjoy genuine freedom. Suggesting that evil is just an unfortunate consequence of an order that otherwise brings us great good does not help the one suffering the misfortune! All of these "arguments" immediately call forth doubt rather than confidence, and few people in the throes of a crisis are much helped by them.

However, there is some merit in this approach insofar as it calls for action alleviating suffering and locates God's presence in those actions. This sounds very much like the carevision that is outlined in this book. But it falls short of carevision in that it does not ground helpful human caregiving in the nature and being of God. To the contrary, in this approach caregiving is provided precisely because God is effectively absent. Caregiving is then a substitute for God's inactivity! But what *religious* help is such caregiving if it is not rooted and established in the love and assistance of God? If human caregiving is offered in spite of God, how can it address the theological questions raised by suffering? It seems that without effective divine agency nothing has been solved regarding the intellectual problem of evil.

Moreover, why bother to pray in this situation? If God is without power to make a difference in the world, what sense can prayer make? Let us suppose we pray to this limited God. What are we to think? God may want to help the sick, but simply doesn't have the resources to bring it off. God may hear the cries of the oppressed, but is helpless to do anything about them. God's heart may be in the right place, but God's hands are tied so far as doing anything useful. For that matter, can we even be assured of God's companionship in our suffering? God may desire to assist us, but not be able. As the human soul struggles for strength, a God of limited power may be unable to rescue such a soul that is overwhelmed by forces of distraction and doubt. God may well promise to help the faithful, but just not have enough clout to deliver on that promise. How can one have courage when dealing with such an impotent God?

As for the idea that God works through the hands of caregivers, how can we be sure it is God and not something else at work? If God lacks power to move people decisively, then we can't be sure care providing has any theological meaning. A powerless God may not be able to get the divine act together sufficiently to direct events in the world. That may also mean we live in potentially the worst possible world, not the best. In a world where God shares power with other forces, erratic and chaotic events may get the upper hand. God's well-meaning plan may be thwarted. God's best simply may not be good enough. How can such a limited God be any consolation and comfort to those who suffer? To talk about such a puny God to the sick and distressed would hardly be good news, and more likely would only deepen despair and hopelessness. Such talk has no solid ground underneath it with which to provide support.

Caregivers would do well to avoid the empty words of the "enfeebled God" argument. Clarence Day writes of his father's tortured faith: "Father expected a good deal of God. He didn't actually accuse God of inefficiency, but when he prayed his tone was loud and angry, like that of a dissatisfied guest in a carelessly managed hotel."[2] A God impotent in the face of evil may be blameless on the issue of suffering, but blameworthy for not being fully God. Those who are sick do not rally in spirit when told the best God can offer them is a shabby hotel. Far better for the care provider to replace the whole game of rational maneuvers with a carevision that reinstates a real God in the universe and a real hope in the heart of the suffering.

Words That Erode God's Goodness

Another type of response to evil is to suggest that it is not inconsistent for a good God to cause or permit human suffering. If God is really God, then God does not have to measure up to any human standard of goodness. Suppose you have witnessed a fire that killed dozens of people. Some of the survivors rail at the heavens: "Where is God when things like this happen?" What are you to say to these spiritually wounded people? One common response is to remind them that what appears evil to us may be good to God. God may have a different standard of goodness, one that does not exclude the suffering of children and innocent people. We may not understand this, but then who can know the mind of God?

In this approach, we must allow the possibility of different standards; otherwise, God would be subordinated to a human standard of goodness. If we expect God to be good according to our standard of goodness, then our standard is supreme rather than God. There would be something greater than God, namely, our notion of goodness to which God must conform. But a God who must answer to something more ultimate is no longer God. The possibilities are: God's Godness (divine freedom) or God's goodness (according to human measure). Isn't it better to retain God and qualify God's goodness, than to lose God altogether?[3]

There is something appealing about this answer to the problem of evil. Who wants a God who can be jerked around by every human idea of what is right and wrong? We all know the excesses that can occur when God is co-opted for every noble cause under the sun! Any God who is worth our time and our worship must be the foundation of morality, not something secondary to it. God must define the good: the good must be precisely what God envisions, intends, commands, and causes to happen.[4] If that God doesn't quite please us, too bad for us.

The only trouble with this approach is that it can lead to a God totally unfit for human fellowship. It is not really better to retain God's Godness at all costs, for if God's goodness is aborted in the process, the price is too high. A heartless God is too severe for religious faith. It is not the case that we must have an absolutely sovereign God or no God at all. While it may cause us some problems to deal with a less than absolutely omnipotent deity, there are far more problems for faith if God is not good in some recognizably human way.

To deny that God is good is to allow the demonic to enter into the very essence of deity. For such a God, nothing is really bad. A God of compromised goodness might be perfectly willing to let the children and innocent suffer horrendous pain. A God who is wishy-washy on goodness might not oppose evil or work for its eradication, but surely talk of this God can only lead to atheism. Contrary to the case in favor of modifying God's goodness, we would sooner have no God at all than an evil God. The proposal of a morally deficient God is a chilling prospect, posing the possibility of a horrifying world order. Omnipotence exercised by a deity uncontrolled by goodness could result in the worst possible world, not the best possible. Absolute power joined to absolute evil can mean only a world of absolute darkness. It is a scenario that leaves us with no grounds for hope whatsoever.

Moreover, this way of grappling with the problem of evil casts the human race into moral madness. Given this God, there would be no reason for human beings to take up any cause that alleviates suffering. Not only is there no theological support for such activism, but it may well be against the divine intent. If it is not in God's will to defeat evil, if it is not clear that God is on the side of goodness, then the whole effort to motivate people to care for one another is undermined. Any religious rationale for action against suffering that negates the will and power of God is fatally flawed. It is a theological argument without a theological foundation. Any theological plan to oppose evil by human effort that is in principle contrary to or even not clearly aligned with the divine intent is doomed from the start.

Caregivers will only experience great embarrassment if they offer those who suffer some form of the "God-above-goodness" argument. In many cases, they are already suffering great doubt about the kindness of God. To say that God must have a plan for a person's affliction or that God may know what we need (pain) better than we do is to cast the sufferer into even deeper despair. It is the theological form of kicking a person when he or she is down. There is no carevision in such a response, no assurance that God is on the side of life and well-being, no effort that escapes the duplicity of a failed faith. There is only confusion and hopelessness. Such words do not help but only wound in soul those already afflicted in body.

Words That Trivialize Evil

In the rock opera *Godspell*, one song has a decidedly theological ring to it. It is a lighthearted spoof of "positive thinking" about personal misfortune and ruin. After listing one catastrophe after another, the lyrics refer to rewards in heaven and counsel that "It's all for the best." The listener is lulled into believing that whatever terrible things happen, there is always a positive meaning to life. Every cloud has a silver lining. "It isn't raining rain you know; it's raining violets." In this approach to the problem of evil, nothing at all is said about the behavior of God. Rather, we try to make the bad things that happen to us really look like good things. The focus in this strategy is on the nature of evil and how to blunt its harsh edge.

The ingenuity of the human mind in denying the reality of evil is truly impressive. Instead of regarding suffering as bad, we look for all kinds of arguments to show that it really is good. One argument is that without evil this world wouldn't be nearly as interesting as it is. The world is like a tapestry, and just as any Rembrandt painting is more appealing for the dark shadows that compose it, so life is better for the evil that is mixed in with the good.

Another blur of the reality of evil is the argument that bad situations are good because evil contributes to building human character. Without a little evil in the world, so the argument goes, we would not be who we are. There would be no occasion for courage, compassion, or sacrifice. We would merely sit around in unchallenged complacency. Since everyone would have what he or she needs, there would be no opportunity for heroism. Since there would be no strife or conflict, there would be no way to grow in moral virtue. Therefore, the world is not worse for the suffering in it, but better! It is a much richer and more interesting place for the evil it contains.

And there is a religious variation on the previous argument. This variation states that if all we experience are sunny skies and open roads we will turn into spiritual dolts. We will develop none of the spiritual qualities essential to the religious quest. If we are never tempted, we will never learn self-control. If we are never set back on our road, we will never learn fortitude and patience. If we never encounter God's silence, we will never appreciate the mystery of our faith. If we never face sorrow and loss, we will have no understanding of the cleansing power of suffering. If we never see the face of death, we will never cling to God in utter dependence. Therefore, the best world for the growth of our soul is a world besieged by evil, a world of development, a world growing toward perfection but not quite there.[5]

This argument that suffering is useful and therefore good is a very popular strategy when dealing with the problem of evil. It is an approach that does not tamper with the transcendence or goodness of God. It also hints of the stuff of which religious heroes are made. To hold on to faith in God in the face of suffering suggests a courageous, resilient spirituality of very high calibre. On the other hand, this approach simply demands too much of the thinking believer. It presents a magic show in which evil or suffering is the main attraction. In this presentation, suffering is part of a disappearing act — "now you see it, now you don't" — that leaves the viewer wondering whether or not such a thing actually exists.

One way this argument tricks us is to conceal the fact that in many cases suffering does *not* lead to any benefits. Many people are not instructed by suffering, are not ennobled by it, and are not led to repentance. Their suffering actually destroys their lives, breaks their spirits, and leads them away from God, not to God. To call suffering good, therefore, is a deception of the worst magnitude.

This utilitarian approach also inverts normal perceptions of what constitutes a good world and a good God when it states that the best world is one with suffering in it. This statement is patently false: such a world is the worst world. The best world, humanly speaking, is one where suffering goes down as happiness goes up. Nor is the God of utilitarianism the best God that could be. While supporters of this argument say a God able to turn evil to good is pretty impressive, those who give some thought to this argument are not impressed. The best God is one who does not use evil for good. It is never morally acceptable deliberately to manufacture or use evil to produce good. Any God who resorts to such a practice is a cruel God, a "cosmic fiend" who shatters the world to teach it a lesson. This God is about as far from the God of the New Testament, who detests evil, does not desire the suffering of the people, and does not send suffering, as one can get.

Any care provider who brings a message of "it's all for the best" to those who suffer is likely to meet a cool reception. Of all the excusing arguments, the utilitarian is the least credible. Those who are sick are quick to pick up on its hypocrisy. It is a word game that tricks our minds into thinking that what is true is really false, what is bad is really good. But those who suffer will not fall for the deception. They will understand that evil is not an illusion, but thinking of it as an illusion is. They will recognize that it is the most insidious of all suggestions to propose that their pain is really a blessing. They will not enter that topsy-turvy world where all benchmarks disappear and all meaning is scrambled. At that point, the care provider can display good sense and good sensitivity by a return to reality and a turn to carevision. Carevision takes suffering with dead seriousness, works on it with a living compassion, and plays no games with its meaning.

Conclusion

Trying to talk our way out of the problem of evil will not work. It is a solution that does not solve anything. A mathematics teacher put a problem on the blackboard and asked if anyone in the class could solve it. One student raised his hand. "I can," he said. Then he walked forward, took an eraser in his hand, looked at the equation for a moment, and erased it from the board. Likewise, attempts to justify the existence of evil merely erase the problem without solving it. They fool us into thinking they provide a solution, but in fact they have only removed the problem from our thinking. Yet we know that the problem is still there.

Caregivers who resort to explanations are likely to increase the level of frustration in their work. Rational efforts that qualify God's power or modify God's goodness or turn bad into good create structures that collapse under their own weight, one pillar at a time. They cry "peace" when there is no peace through them. Words offered to soothe the suffering have no authority, as Daniel Simundson reminds us: "All intellectual answers sound hollow and insufficient to the person still in the trauma of great suffering."[6]

An ancient rule of the Talmud says that we should not visit those who are sick with eye disease and headaches because speech is injurious to such people.[7] If you have ever felt helpless and unable to talk your way out of the awful pain of suffering, the wisdom in this instruction is clear. Theodicies are useless medicine for those who do not want rationalizations but relief. Care providers will soon realize that arguments are not the therapy needed, but something else, something with substance, that replaces argument with action. That something is carevision, as we will see next.

CHAPTER THREE

The Turn to Action

The fact that words may be empty comfort for the sick does not necessarily establish action as a legitimate strategy for dealing with the intellectual problem of evil. To make that point requires some attention to the importance of action in solving the problem of evil. In this chapter we will turn our focus to that issue.

Doing Something About Suffering

Carevision is an activist solution to the problem of evil. While it does not totally eliminate the importance of words, as we will shortly see, its focus is on *doing* something about suffering as a way of *saying* something about the intellectual problem of evil. It is *care* with a vision of its potential impact on the question of meaning. It is a *vision* of the uncertainty and anguish of the human soul therapeutically addressed by action that alleviates suffering. Carevision is a strategy for those whose eyes are lifted to the ultimate questions of life while their feet are firmly planted in the tasks of making life more livable. It is vision tempered by action that is informed by spirituality.

Harold Kushner writes about a Jewish mourning ritual called the meal of replenishment: "On returning from the cemetery, the mourner is not supposed to take food for himself (or to serve others). Other people have to feed him, symbolizing the way the community rallies around him to sustain him and to try to fill the emptiness in his world."[1] In this beautiful ritual we see carevision at work. Instead of sitting around discussing the justice of God, the mourning community acts in a most fundamental way to help the grieving person. It serves one of the most basic needs of human survival, the need for nourishment. In their action, the mourning community says something about the God who supplies our physical and spiritual needs as a way to rescue us from suffering.

The turn to action as a way to deal with suffering has good precedent. It may be that a kind of carevision was present even in the time of Jesus. Among the many stories of action taken to relieve suffering there is one that portrays Jesus commending the carevision of one of his contemporaries. Or, at least, Kosuke Koyama understands it this way. The cure of the Canaanite woman's daughter (Matt. 15:21-28) is often interpreted as a theological lesson about faith that prevails in spite of resistance and disappointment. Koyama, however, focuses on the love of the woman for her daughter and the woman's concern for her daughter's health. Koyama says it was this compassionate care for wholeness that led to the woman's faith in Jesus.[2] If so, then the faith Jesus commends is a faith characterized by carevision, a faith that tackles the problem of evil by acting to relieve suffering. The woman had faith that something could be done, believed Jesus could do it, and brought her daughter to Jesus for healing. Jesus' actual cure of the girl is an affirmation of the mother's carevision.

Voices for a Practical Theodicy

Increasingly, writers who ponder the problem of evil are turning to carevision as a possible solution. In many early theodicies, carevision is a theme within a more extensive proposal for dealing with the problem of evil. Over fifty years ago, Jesuit philosopher M. C. D'Arcy wrote a book that explored the issue in the problem of evil by way of an imaginative dialogue. Through the voices in the debate, D'Arcy made the point that God abhors pain and evil as much as we do, and wants to defeat it. He admonished his readers to fight evil rather than curse God.[3] Anglican philosopher Cyril Joad affirmed a dualism of good and evil and a personal God who assists in the struggle against evil.[4]

Other writers turned to the action of God who overcomes evil through Christ on the cross, including J. S. Whale, who argued that the Christian answer to evil is not intellectual but practical: that is, God defeats sin and death on the cross, both reconciling and rescuing us.[5] Insisting that "the only full solution of evil is the overcoming of it," clergyman-philosopher Nels Ferré focused on moral evil and the effectiveness of the cross in defeating sin.[6] A more inclusive proposal was offered by theologian Edwin Lewis, who argued that God does battle against all uncreative, demonic forces in the world by suffering within the creative process and on the cross. The resurrection of Christ is the believer's assurance that God has the power to overcome evil.[7] Similarly, Oxford theologian Austin Farrer argued that God defeats evil and overrules it by drawing divine purposes out of natural processes, as in, for example, Christ's redemptive suffering and victorious benefits.[8] The suggestion that we should turn to God as a saving power rather than an explanatory cause was developed by theologian and preacher George Buttrick. He suggested that the problem is existential and requires a *breakthrough* or *event* for its resolution. The resurrection of Jesus is such an event that defeats all levels of evil.[9]

In more recent times, some writers have focused directly on the importance of human action in dealing with the intellectual problem of evil. In her classic work, *Suffering*, theologian Dorothee Soelle commends a devotion of imitating Christ in suffering, but emphasizes the necessity to reduce suffering. We are not to try to explain suffering, but to act in order to get out from under its burden. The issue for Soelle is not making sense of suffering but activating people to stand and work against suffering.[10]

A similar tack is taken by John Roth, who argues that the Jesus of Christianity overcame evil and so should we. The way ahead is to follow Jesus in defying all that wastes life. The resolution of the problem of suffering can be in this life as Christians do battle against evil wherever they find it in the world.[11]

Philosopher Kenneth Surin rejects contemporary theoretical theodicies in favor of practical theodicies that offer a cure rather than an answer. With unjust or meaningless suffering, "only the abatement and the abolition of the agony will constitute an adequate 'answer.'"[12] Religion professor Wendy Farley echoes that judgment in her essay proposing an active compassion that struggles against evil rather than the development of any theory that justifies suffering.[13]

The Development of Carevision

Two comments will help to set the direction for our thinking about carevision as a resource for dealing with the problem of evil. Dennis Saylor writes that when it comes to caring for the suffering, we "should not pretend to know how their particular loss fits into a plan of Divine reason and purpose. Know only that on this side of Heaven, it hurts and a ministry of comfort is needed."[14] John Cobb describes this "ministry of comfort" in terms of pastoral care: "Many pastors have decided that it is better not to try to give any answer at all. The pastor's task is to be present with the sufferer, to 'hear' her or him, to let the parishioner know that the fear, anger, and loneliness that are felt can be expressed and will be accepted."[15]

Active presence with those who suffer is one kind of "ministry of comfort" that can alleviate pain. There are many others, and we will look at a few later in this book. The important point is to recognize that such action has far-reaching implications for the problem of evil. It provides relief not only for physical pain, but for spiritual wounds as well. The problem of suffering cannot be neatly divided into practical and theoretical aspects, for the practical and the theoretical intermingle and interact.

We know that what people think is an important factor in the practical management of suffering. But more to the point, when we do something to assist those who are suffering and we do this with some spiritual weight, we make a statement about the ultimate nature of things, about God, and about the real truth of the problem of evil. We say, for instance, that suffering is not an implacable tyrant, pain is not the last word, and injustice is not the rule. Rather, action overcoming suffering signals an altogether different order struggling to come into prominence. It casts the problem of evil in an altogether new light, where there is love, vision, care, relief, and hope.

An event from popular culture can illustrate the power of actions to speak. In the drama *The Dead Poets Society*, John Keating, an unconventional prep school English teacher, encourages his students to find their individuality, express themselves, and swim against the stream. He invites them to call him "captain," and marches them to the front of the room and the top of his desk as a lesson in seeing things in a different way. With his clarion call, "Seize the moment," ringing in their ears, many members of the class discover the courage to do the things they really wished to do, but were to afraid to try. Unfortunately, one of the students, caught up in a struggle with an authoritarian and abusive father, commits suicide. Keating is made the scapegoat for the tragedy and asked to leave.

In the closing scene of the drama, the loyalty of his students is powerfully portrayed. As he returns to his room to collect his belongings, he finds the schoolmaster in charge, and a sad, grim-faced class. Just as he is about to leave, one student triumphantly leaps to his feet next to his desk, then climbs to the top of his desk facing his captain. Then another student bolts to his desktop, and another. As the master struggles to regain order, more students step to their desktops. The camera focuses on their silent but intense faces, all fixed on their leader and liberator. Surprised yet satisfied by this silent, powerful statement, Keating thanks the boys and departs from the room.

The expressive power of action that helps suffering people is no less dramatic. The faithful, sensitive, productive care given to one who suffers is a "body language" that shouts a message to the receiver of care. When administered with religious vision, it is a sacrament conveying a message through the hands and the smiles, the foot baths and the prayers of the caregiver. It is love made luminous, grace with form and shape, spirit made flesh. Action helping others is the physical instrument that makes the invisible visible, the unseen stand out. Things of mystery that no one could say in words are expressed through the therapies, services, and kindnesses of the care provider. In the beginning of all effective responses to the problem of evil is the *act*.

Conclusion

We have looked at the trouble with words and suggested the power of action when dealing with the problem of evil. We must now back up slightly and offer a qualification. The saying "actions speak more loudly than words" does not eliminate words altogether, but only places actions in a more prominent role. While some theodicies may not speak comfortingly at all, that does not mean all words about suffering are without comfort. There is one word that is not empty, and that is the word based on revelation. Before the human act there was God's act: in the beginning was the Word.

Attention to the words of revelation must not be misunderstood as a resort to rational theodicies, however. Quite the opposite. It is important to look at the biblical record for its story of divine assistance in alleviating suffering. There we see that God also deals with evil by helping people overcome it. That word speaks comfortingly to the suffering when it operates as a foundation for an active ministry of comfort. Of course, one aspect of that active ministry would be to share the biblical stories with those who suffer.

Nothing in an activist approach to the problem of evil disallows the importance of such positive messages. Indeed, as we will see, it is just such religious content that gives action its theological worth. The crucial element in an activist approach, nevertheless, is the work done to overcome suffering. The word of revelation is the foundation upon which this caregiving is built, and the action of providing care is the substance that gives meaning to the biblical stories and counsels. In carevision, action has a strong theological foundation, and the religious stories are given effective, practical application.

PART TWO

Biblical Foundations for Carevision

CHAPTER FOUR

The Mighty Acts of God

"Where are you coming from?" someone may question us, trying to figure out our basic point of view. It is an important question because it drives us to confront our assumptions, perspectives, and prejudices. Carevision also comes from a certain set of presuppositions and principles. It is predicated on the biblical story of God's treatment of evil. That story gives carevision its religious soul and style. It is the arena where many of the issues in the problem of evil surface and are addressed.

We have seen that many rationalizations of the problem of evil cannot deliver what they promise. They also do not capture the fullness of the Christian faith. These facts became clear to me while visiting a terminally ill woman in my community. A devout member of a local church, she possessed a stalwart faith and courageous devotion. Over the course of her lengthy illness we had prayed together many times. Now we faced the last enemy. What words could I say to kindle an honest hope? As so often before, the rugged faith of that tried-and-true pilgrim came to the rescue. Near her bed was a sign that read, "God is greater than any problem you have." For this woman, the solution to her suffering was not in any human words of comfort, but in the power of God. While theodicies might fail, God would not.

God's action in overcoming evil is at the heart of the biblical way of handling the problem of evil. It is predicated on the assumption that God's goodness entails an interest in human welfare. In particular, it assumes that human welfare and happiness go up as pain goes down.[1] The sympathies of the God of faith are with the sufferer. Not only that, the God we meet in the Bible votes for the side that is eliminating suffering. When Jesus assured the disciples, "Take courage; I have conquered the world!" (John 16:33), he was summing up the whole of his ministry and of God's will in terms of victory over evil. It is the style of God to overcome the suffering of the world, not to compromise with it or utilize it for good. How this happens according to the biblical story, and the implications of this action, are the subject of this and the next three chapters, as we consider four themes: God as a warrior against evil, Jesus' campaign against Satan, the miracle stories in the New Testament, and the victory of resurrection.

God, a Warrior Against Evil

The God of the Bible is a mighty God who takes action against evil. God has the power and goodness to overcome the most intense, protracted suffering. The ancient writer exults: "Yours, O LORD, are the greatness, the power, the glory, the victory, and the majesty; for all that is in the heavens and on the earth is yours" (1 Chron. 29:11). Unlike mere mortals, God has qualities that uniquely equip God for the task of taking on evil. God is eternal, unlimited by time (Gen. 1:1; Isa. 44:6; Job 38:33), and omnipresent, overflowing the boundaries of space (1 Kings 8:27; Matt. 28:20; Acts 17:24). Most significantly, God is not intimidated by the forces of evil. With perfect power to accomplish God's will (Pss. 33:9, 115:3), nothing is impossible for God (Luke 1:37; Matt. 19:26).

God is also loving. In praise of God's protective care, the psalmist sings, "O taste and see that the LORD is good!" (34:8). God has the best interests of Israel at heart. God loves Israel like a groom loves his bride, a mother her child, and a father his son. God wants to rescue the people from destruction and shower on them the blessings of salvation (Isa. 45:8, 46:13, 51:5-6; Rom. 11:26). In Jesus, God goes about doing good to those he encounters (Luke 7:18-23). The welfare of the people is one of God's foremost concerns, if not *the* foremost concern (Luke 12:22-34; Acts 14:17). God's loving-kindness is absolutely to be trusted. It is a steadfast love that "endures forever" (Ps. 106:1), a certainty about which there is "no variation or shadow due to change" (James 1:17).

The power and love of God meet in a paradoxical way in a third divine attribute, justice. When the people turn from God's covenant to ways of idolatry, immorality, and social irresponsibility, God's righteousness breaks out as wrath (Isa. 5:24ff.; Jer. 6:11; Rom. 1:18).[2] God is passionately on the side of the poor and the needy, and levels one scathing barrage after another at those who neglect them: "For three transgressions of Israel . . . I will not revoke the punishment; because they sell the righteous for silver, and the needy for a pair of sandals—they who trample the head of the poor into the dust of the earth, and push the afflicted out of the way" (Amos 2:6-7). The wrath of God is a terrible flame and sword (Isa. 10:16-17; Ezek. 21:10) that punishes and destroys the wicked (Hos. 9:7; Isa. 1:19-20). While God's power is instrumental in this terrible suffering, God's love shines through these awful events. God's wrath is always expressed in the context of God's love (Hos. 11). It is not a capricious, blind rage, but an extension of the covenant care of God. "It is he who has torn, and he will heal us," comforts Hosea (6:1). God takes no pleasure in administering harsh justice (Ezek. 18:32), but wishes above all that Israel live and prosper under the covenant (Amos 4; Isa. 1:26, 10:20). Therefore, even the wrath of God ultimately serves the love of God, and the divine purpose in overcoming evil.

That God is first and foremost a loving God is most clearly evident when that love breaks out as mercy. The psalmist says it beautifully: "But you, O Lord, are a God merciful and gracious, slow to anger and abounding in steadfast love and faithfulness" (86:15). "As a father has compassion for his children, so the LORD has compassion for those who fear him" (103:13). God's disciplining is only "for a brief moment" (Isa. 54:7-9), and God's anger is never permanent (Ps. 103:9). God tempers wrath with mercy (Jer. 3:12-14), and withholds punishment from the repentant (Jer. 18:7-8). In Jesus, God's love is so extraordinary that it forgives sin whether it brings harm to others or to God (Luke 5:20, 23:34). So great is the love of God that while God calls others to reduce suffering, even those who do not heed the call can find forgiveness.

This God mighty in power and love applies all the divine weight to smothering out evil and suffering. This is evident from the very beginning, when God "gathered the waters of the sea as in a bottle" and "put the deeps in storehouses" (Ps. 33:7). God pushed back the surrounding chaos in order to make a world (Gen. 1:2). God turned chaos back for order, overcame bad for good (Isa. 45:18). Not only that, God continues to hold back the forces of destruction (Isa. 51:9-11; Pss. 74:12-14, 89:6-11), thereby assuring the dominion of good.[3]

God is a champion for the people of Israel, taking them by the hand (Isa. 42:5-7) and guiding them just as shepherds watch their flocks (Ezek. 34:11-16). God protects the innocent and poor, and tells all people how to live in God's favor: "He has told you, O mortal, what is good; and what does the Lord require of you but to do justice, and to love kindness, and to walk humbly with your God?" (Micah 6:8). Most interesting, God saves Israel from her foreign enemies (Exod. 14) until Israel goes too far afield. Then God utilizes the alien nations to bring Israel back to the covenant context (Amos 3:11; Hos. 10:10; Isa. 9:11, 10:5, 13:4, 41:25).

Whatever the actual record of God's victory over evil in the world, the prophets assure the people of a future peaceable kingdom brought in by God: "They shall beat their swords into plowshares, and their spears into pruning hooks; nation shall not lift up sword against nation, neither shall they learn war any more" (Isa. 2:4). The recovery of Israel will be like a dead man rising from the grave who is restored to life by the breath of God (Ezek. 37:1-14). Full triumph of God over evil is promised to the followers of Jesus. In the life everlasting, there will be rewards, blessings, and joy (Mark 10:29-30; Matt. 5:1-12). Indeed, these blessings will be so great that the faithful will forget the pain of their earthly life (John 16:20-21).

The Laments

The recital of God's marvelous deeds in overcoming evil is complemented by another theme in the Bible, especially in the Old Testament, of pouring out one's complaint to God. Though relatively minor, this theme is of great importance for caregivers, who may frequently encounter this cry of protest or the recital of a grievance before God. The plaintive cry of the psalmist, "I pour out my complaint before him" (142:2), constitutes a seldom recognized stream of piety in the Bible. I would argue that this note in Scripture is the human response to a deity perceived to be powerful and good, but somehow inactive for the time being. It is the human, heavenward counterpart of the divine, earthward revelation of God's mighty acts overcoming evil.

That is to say, the faithful of the Old Testament would not talk back to God if they did not believe that God is powerfully active in the battle to alleviate suffering. The underlying assumption of their plea to God is a belief that God is able and wants to do something about their plight. Thus, when Abraham bargains with God on behalf of Sodom and Gomorrah (Gen. 18:23-25), Abraham's assumption is that God is a reasonable, good, and capable God. The reason for the plea is that God seems to be acting contrary to God's basic character. God was perceived as a God with sufficient goodness and power to be able to win a few for the side of righteousness.[4]

A similar dynamic seems to be operating in the situation of Job. With passionate disappointment, Job complains to God about God's unfair treatment of the innocent (9:22-24). In particular, he protests that God has made him God's target (7:20). In wrath God has torn Job (16:9), pursued and oppressed him (19:22). This is altogether puzzling and distressing to Job because he assumes that God has the power and the goodness to maintain a just world: "If it is a contest of strength, he is the strong one! If it is a matter of justice, who can summon him?" (9:19). Job asks why the world does not conform to the moral order that he assumes is integral to the divine nature (21:19-26).

Job is confident that if he could just get an audience with God, things could be straightened out (13:3). The problem is that God is somehow silent and inactive at the moment (19:7). Job is perplexed because God doesn't *do* anything for the oppressed: "God pays no attention to their prayer" (24:12). Job assumes that God would act with justice and power, if only God would listen, so he cries out: "Oh, that I knew where I might find him, that I might come even to his dwelling! I would lay my case before him, and fill my mouth with arguments" (23:3-4). Job can be so bold because he is confident that God is great and God is good. His protest stems from his deep-rooted faith in a God who wishes, and is powerful enough, to make a world without pain.

This belief in the might and will of God to overcome evil is also mirrored in many of the psalms. God's power and goodness is joyously celebrated in the psalms of thanksgiving and praise (Pss. 9, 30, 124, 136, 138, 145-150). The psalms of lament speak even more clearly of God's power and will to save people from their suffering. These psalms were written by people suffering under afflictions of various sorts, ranging from physical sickness (Ps. 6) to persecution from community members (Ps. 3), and including trials to the whole nation (Ps. 74). As with Abraham and Job, the psalmists confess a deep faith in God's power and goodness by expressing perplexity with God for not doing a better job in the world. The lament psalms are plaintive grievances that arise out of a strong conviction of God's sovereignty and benevolence. It is just because of that faith that the psalmists are so upset, pleading with God to *do* something: "Do not be silent" (Ps. 109:1), "Rescue me" (Ps. 71:4), "Make haste to help me" (Ps. 40:13).

The psalmists write out of a strong conviction and experience of God's control over the world and God's good will for the people. Although the context is not perfectly clear, some of the psalms are written against the background of actual divine assistance already received: "The LORD has done great things for us, and we rejoiced (Ps. 126:3; see also Pss. 3:7, 13:6, 22:4-5, 31:6-8, 71:19). More often, the psalmist expresses confidence that God will help in due time: "All my enemies shall be ashamed and struck with terror; they shall turn back, and in a moment be put to shame" (Ps. 6:10; see also Pss. 5:12, 10:17, 57:3, 59:10). Some of the psalms seem to express a confidence in God *in the midst* of the suffering, leaving uncertain the time when relief will be forthcoming: "The LORD is my strength and my shield; in him my heart trusts; so I am helped, and my heart exults, and with my song I give thanks to him" (Ps. 28:7; see also Ps. 42:11). In any case, all of these psalms of lament proclaim a God who renders or will render practical assistance to the afflicted. They report that something has happened or will happen to relieve the very real pain of the writer. There is no doubt about God's power and goodness to rectify the situation.

The poignancy of the lament psalms turns on just this expectation. It is just because of a strong faith in God that the lament arises. The perplexity that occurs when God does not act according to God's nature causes excruciating spiritual distress: "Is your steadfast love declared in the grave, or your faithfulness in Abaddon? Are your wonders known in the darkness, or your saving help in the land of forgetfulness?" (Ps. 88:11-12). In this most somber of all the psalms, the dark cloud is caused by confusion over the divine activity. How are God's love, faithfulness, or wonders shown forth in the current suffering of the psalmist?

If the psalmist did not presume that God is great and good there would be no difficulty. It is precisely because of the high faith of the psalmist that high expectations of God develop. These high expectations, when measured against the cruel reality of evil, precipitate insistent, even strident, pleas for help: "Give ear to my prayer, O God; do not hide yourself from my supplication. Attend to me, and answer me" (Ps. 55:1-2). Who could talk to God like that but one with a noble faith, one with grand expectations that seem to have been dashed to the ground? The lament psalms tell of a deep faith wounded by the adversity that has befallen the writer. The distress is so great that, try as they may, the afflicted can no longer keep silent, but are compelled to speak (Ps. 39:2-3).

The psalmists' tribute to God's sovereignty and goodness is unmistakable. God *has* done great things (Pss. 44:1-2, 71:19). God *is* great, doing wondrous things (Ps. 86:10). God *will* establish the righteous (Ps. 7:9), and will ultimately triumph (Ps. 3:8). God is not a "God who delights in wickedness" (Ps. 5:4), but a God who is "good and forgiving, abounding in steadfast love to all who call" (Ps. 86:5). Being good, God would not knowingly permit the people to suffer (Ps. 44:24). Rather, God will "send forth his steadfast love" (Ps. 57:3) to save the oppressed (Ps. 109:26). Where there is extended suffering, the foremost question is, "Has his steadfast love ceased forever?" (Ps. 77:8).

The issue for the psalmists is not whether God has the will or the wherewithal to overcome evil. The issue is God's present silence or absence. The pleas of the psalmists are not for God to somehow change God's being, but to activate what is already there. So the psalmist asks, "Why, O Lord, do you stand far off? . . . Rise up, O Lord; O God, lift up your hand" (Ps. 10:1,12; see also Pss. 7:6, 59:4, 74:22). The psalmist pleads with God not only to wake up but also to come out of hiding and to rescue him (Ps. 144:5-7). The psalmist also asks God to speak up, to become active about solving the problem. Faced with the awful distance of God, the psalmist prays, "O God, do not keep silence; do not hold your peace or be still, O God!" (Ps. 83:1; see also Ps. 109:1).

All these cries for help come to one thing: a plea to God to enter the arena of human struggle and to fight against the oppressors, finally vindicating the afflicted (Ps. 35:1,24). The psalmists have no doubt about God's ability to understand the situation or about God's power: "But you do see! Indeed you note trouble and grief" (Ps. 10:14), and "God my King is from old, working salvation in the earth" (Ps. 74:12). The psalmists also have no doubt about God's goodness: "O how abundant is your goodness that you have laid up for those who fear you" (Ps. 31:19). The psalmists only ask that God act on God's character, and be the deliverer the psalmists believe God to be.

The final word in the Psalms on suffering is a word of trust that God will act to alleviate pain. The psalmists are sure God will deal with the problem of evil by easing their suffering. They reflect this faith in their frequent descriptions of God as the one who helps. "Hear, O LORD, and be gracious to me! O LORD, be my helper!" is followed by a description of how God has assisted the psalmist (Ps. 30:10ff.). And God is praised as the psalmists' strength and advocate: "But surely, God is my helper; the Lord is the upholder of my life" (Ps. 54:4); "I will lift up my eyes to the hills — from where will my help come? My help comes from the LORD, who made heaven and earth" (Ps. 121:1-2). The lament psalms breath a vibrant faith that God can make a real difference with real suffering.[5]

Issues

The biblical account of God's intent and action against evil and the human expectation of God's justice and care avoid several issues that plague treatments of the problem of evil. For one, focusing on divine action against evil avoids the appeal to mystery sometimes advanced by apologists. It is sometimes argued that the existence of evil proves that if there is a God, God chooses to evade our understanding and confound our theology. God's ways remain beyond our scrutiny, hidden in a cloud of mystery.[6] We simply cannot know why there is evil in the world, or what God is up to in allowing it to exist.

The appeal to mystery is the polar opposite of the biblical record, where God's will and ways are clearly opposed to evil. It is also an answer that does not answer. While an appeal to mystery is an appropriate statement of Christian piety, it is inadequate as a strategy for Christian thought. Any approach that forces believers to preserve their hearts while losing their minds is unacceptable. Any solution to the problem of evil that bypasses all understanding sidesteps the problem rather than engages it. Instead of joining up with the biblical God in a battle against the forces of evil, one has simply given up the struggle by making a "white flag" surrender.[7] An appeal to the mystery of God's ways only adds one more layer of complexity that needs to be explained.

A second difficulty that the biblical account avoids is the effort to wriggle out of the problem by appeal to God's companionable suffering. It is sometimes suggested that the way God deals with suffering is to bear it with us. God is the fellow sufferer who in every way carries the weight of our humanity, even to the point of enduring death on a cross.[8] It is God's heart that breaks first in the midst of wrenching loss.[9] The identification of God with human pain means we can't blame God for suffering, but must admire and reverence God for the divine empathy.

While the image of a suffering God holds profound religious meaning and is not to be taken lightly, it is hardly an answer to the problem of human suffering. John Roth finds little comfort in this approach: "For if a suffering God is only a suffering God, then God help us."[10] While the picture of a God who does not require of us anything God is not willing to endure is religiously uplifting, there is a sobering side to that image. The cross may also be a symbol of the weakness of God, God's death or helplessness in the face of evil.[11] In that case we can only grieve over the suffering of God, not only in sympathy for God, but in despair for ourselves. A God who suffers with us but does not take up the battle against evil and help us, is a small consolation.[12]

Ronald Goetz draws this disturbing conclusion from the notion of a limited God: "To my mind, any concept of a limited deity finally entails a denial of the capacity of God to redeem the world, and thus, ironically, raises the question of whether God is in the last analysis even love, at least love in the Christian sense of the term." For Goetz, any valid notion of a suffering God "must show how God's suffering mitigates evil." And more strongly still: "The mere fact of God's suffering doesn't solve the question; it exacerbates it."[13]

An appeal to God's suffering for an answer to the problem of evil also presents a truncated view of the Christian drama of the cross and resurrection of Jesus. It is a view that is fixated at the cross and fails to include the resurrection. It is similar in style to some writers who argue that the cross is the center and norm of Christian faith and life.[14] But any Christian theology in which Easter is swallowed up by Good Friday is a partial theology at best. The cross is incomplete without Easter.[15] Similarly, views of divine involvement that conclude with the suffering of God and ignore the triumph of God over evil are inadequate. The hope of the Christian faith is that God overcomes evil in the glorious victory of the resurrection, not that the cross is the final word of salvation.[16]

CHAPTER FIVE

The Devil and All His Ways

The struggle of God against evil comes to sharp focus in the New Testament, where the lines of opposition are clearly drawn. On the one side, evil becomes personified in an arch-demon, the devil. On the other side, divine action that alleviates suffering takes on incarnate shape in the person of Jesus Christ. Much of the Christian drama concerns the contest between these two figures. We are here concentrating on the offensive of Jesus against the devil and all his evil ways.

But that is not the whole story of the biblical campaign to lessen human suffering. In the lobby of the Johns Hopkins University Hospital in Baltimore, Maryland, a larger-than-life statue of Jesus, with hands stretched out to receive the sick and afflicted, greets those who come for help. That statue accurately captures the life and ministry of one who gave living form to God's love. It conveys the fact that Jesus devoted considerable time to serving the disturbed, the diseased, and the dying. This healing and helping work can be clustered around three topics: the devil and his evil ways; the miraculous cure of pain, illness, and disability; and raisings from the dead, including Jesus' own victory over the grave. We will consider the first of these topics in this chapter, and the others in the following two.

The Evil Doings of the Devil

A *Far Side* cartoon pictures a devil in hell poking a pitchfork in the back of a hapless new tenant. The victim stands before two doors. On the one is written, "Damned if you do," on the other, "Damned if you don't." The devil urges, "C'mon, C'mon — its either one or the other."[1]

Known for their cynicism and dark humor, Gary Larson's cartoons often reflect the mind of popular culture. Although we may not have a clue as to the source of suffering, more often than not, the devil is singled out as a likely culprit. Interestingly, this also seems to be the approach in the New Testament. Although it is little help in figuring out the source of evil, the Bible is quite willing to blame the devil for much of what goes wrong with the world.

However, where this devil comes from is not quite so clear. By appealing to widely divergent texts, some readers of the Bible argue that the devil can be traced back to a fallen angel (Ezek. 28:12-17; Isa. 14:12-14; Luke 10:18; Rev. 12:7-9) cast down because of pride and rebellion. This dubious detective work is little help in explaining the source of evil, since the most primitive devil is God's colleague (Zech. 3:1; Job 1:12).

The notion of a sinister being that causes all kinds of trouble for human beings seems to have developed sometime around the third century B.C., possibly in response to the trials that had befallen the nation of Israel.[2] At that time, the notion of a truly evil devil appears as a cosmic force opposed to and by God (Ps. 74:14), and as a dragon or serpent-like creature variously called "the serpent" (Gen. 3:4-5), "Leviathan" (Isa. 27:1), and "Rahab" (Isa. 51:9).

Whatever the origin of the notion of a devil or the name *Satan,* it is clear that this being is harmful, causing suffering or evil of all kinds. The devil is a deceiver (Gen. 3:1-7) and liar (John 8:44) in his dealings with human beings. The devil brings on spiritual anguish by leading people into sin (Matt. 4:3; 1 John 3:8-10). An enemy of the word of salvation (Luke 8:12), the devil has "blinded the minds of the unbelievers, to keep them from seeing the light of the gospel of the glory of Christ, who is the image of God" (2 Cor. 4:4). He is "like a roaring lion," seeking someone to "devour" (1 Pet. 5:8). The "wiles of the devil" (Eph. 6:11) oppose the work of the kingdom (2 Thess. 2:4), and are a "snare" to the life of the faithful (1 Tim. 3:7).

The devil poisons human relationships by leading people to lie (Acts 5:3). The devil is an unclean spirit that enters persons to destroy them (Mark 1:23-24) and a raging demon who drives people crazy (Mark 5:1-20). He is a pathological power who can strike people blind and dumb (Matt. 12:22); indeed, all manner of bodily afflictions can be attributed to him (2 Cor. 12:7). The devil holds in his hands the most fearsome of all powers, the power of death (Heb. 2:14). Portrayed as a most loathsome creature by medieval artists, the devil is a horror fantasy come true. There is no kind or degree of suffering that is beyond his power to inflict on people.

Jesus' Campaign Against Satan

Just as suffering is identified with the devil, the life and ministry of Jesus is characterized by his struggle "against the rulers, against the authorities, against the cosmic powers of this present darkness, against the spiritual forces of evil in the heavenly places" (Eph. 6:12). This opposition is evident at the very beginning of Jesus' ministry, when the devil tempted Jesus to prove he was the Son of God by performing certain miracles and acts of obedience (Luke 4:1-13).

As he did with God and God's servant Job, the tempter tried to bargain with Jesus, so that Jesus might compromise his ministry and the devil might gain power over him. The devil first challenged Jesus to prove his divinity by turning stones to bread. In reply, Jesus cited Scripture: "One does not live by bread alone." Next, the devil offered Jesus power over all the kingdoms of the world, if Jesus would only worship him. Confirming his obedience to God alone, Jesus again turned back the offer. Finally, the devil asked that Jesus jump from the pinnacle of the temple to prove that he is the Son of God, but again Jesus summoned the Scripture that forbids anyone to "put the Lord your God to the test." In spite of the great appeal of the devil's offers,[3] Jesus did not fall for his ways, but remained resolutely opposed to his scheme.

When accused, Jesus denied being in league with the devil (Matt. 12:22-27), and taught his followers to pray for deliverance from evil (Matt. 6:13). More decisively, his mission was to "destroy the works of the devil" (1 John 3:8), an assignment dramatically illustrated in his treatment of the Gerasene demoniac (Mark 5:1-20). In this frightening story, the evil of the demonic world is borne by the man Jesus confronted. Crazed in mind, he ran among the tombs terrifying all who came near to him. Jesus, however, showed no fear in the presence of this fierce and dangerous man. Rather, Jesus confronted him directly and ordered the demon out of him. The evil spirit, who was actually many spirits, begged to be transferred to a herd of swine nearby. Jesus complied with the demon's request, and the pigs, whipped to a frenzy by the evil spirits, plunged into the sea and drowned, taking their ugly demons with them. When the people came out to see what had happened, they found Jesus and the demoniac sitting there, the latter, "clothed and in his right mind."

The kingdom that Jesus inaugurated marked the beginning of the end of the rule of Satan on earth. This is evident in the healing miracles Jesus performed. Jesus spent a great deal of his ministry casting out the cohorts of the devil, the spirits and demons that do the devil's work (Mark 3:11; Matt. 9:32-33; Luke 7:21). The final showdown with the devil occurred in Jesus' struggle on the cross. On the cross, Jesus erased "the record that stood against us with its legal demands. He set this aside, nailing it to the cross. He disarmed the rulers and authorities and made a public example of them, triumphing over them" (Col. 2:14-15). The cross is God's action in defeating the devil. It is the dramatic encounter between God and the devil that ends in the devil's defeat.[4] The sign of this victory is the resurrection of Jesus Christ in which God "raised him from the dead and seated him at his right hand in the heavenly places, far above all rule and authority and power and dominion, and above every name that is named" (Eph. 1:20-21).

Jesus does not bargain with the devil, but contends against him, and utterly defeats him. While the devil still has a place in the world, his rule is fading (1 Cor. 2:6). In spite of his presence, Satan has no power over Christ (John 14:30). It is only a matter of time before his total demise and defeat (Luke 10:18; Rev. 12:10) under the rule of Christ, who "must reign until he has put all his enemies under his feet" (1 Cor. 15:25). Then the devil will go into the eternal fire prepared for him and all his companions (Matt. 25:41).

According to the Bible, then, God the warrior against evil,

mighty in power, triumphs gloriously, shattering the enemy (Exod. 15) and giving his followers reason to sing with Martin Luther:

> Though hordes of devils fill the land
> All threat'ning to devour us,
> We tremble not, unmoved we stand;
> They cannot overpow'r us.
> This world's prince may rage,
> In fierce war engage.
> He is doomed to fail;
> God's judgment must prevail!
> One little word subdues him.[5]

The Devil Made Me Do It?

In a book published in 1953, Rudolph Bultmann wrote, "Man's knowledge and mastery of the world have advanced to such an extent through science and technology that it is no longer possible for anyone seriously to hold the New Testament view of the world."[6] Included in the things we could no longer believe, Bultmann said, is the whole spirit world with its demons and arch-devil, Satan. Recently, a pastor and professor of religion commented, "It is fair to say that from that day in 1955 when I entered higher education, I never again encountered anyone teaching Bible who affirmed that the world is as the Bible says it is."[7] We can assume this includes what the Bible says about evil spirits.

In view of modern science and cultural sophistication, what are we to make of the biblical stories about the devil and all his evil ways? Surely we cannot turn back the clock of modern investigation and learning to a time before enlightened understanding. Our situation is like that of the child who is about to take her first steps. Once she stands up to walk, she is committed for life. Once we are set on the path of reason, we are committed for life. If we have simpler, more reasonable ways to explain behavior and events, we should consider them. The trouble is that these methods of explanation do not satisfy in all cases.

Richard Vieth has written about three expressions of social evil of particularly horrifying dimensions.[8] During World War II, Nazi doctors participated in the mass murder of millions of Jews, supervising the killing of as many as ten thousand persons a day in the gas chambers. In 1960, Stanley Milgram began a series of experiments that proved that even though it is against their better judgment, people may continue to inflict pain if they are instructed to do so by an authority figure. And in 1968, a task force of soldiers slaughtered between five and six hundred unarmed civilians at My Lai, Vietnam.

While pointing out that all these events were fueled by human perversity,[9] Vieth notes the way the various factors contributing to the end result can take on a life of their own, hurling their human instruments to the tragic final action. Evil can become incarnate in "ideologies, movements, and institutions." These materializations and great destructive social configurations can function like "gods" to the people, similar to the "principalities and powers" in the New Testament, the demonic forces sometimes called Satan, that oppose God's will. In this way, our "ideologies, social structures, and psychological patterns" can have "demonic potential." Perhaps this is something of what those fifty percent of the population in 1973 recognized when they admitted to personal belief in Satan.[10]

The issue of whether or not Satan as a being exists today does not weaken the importance of the story of Jesus' battle against Satan in his day. In that battle, we see a divine intention, and a pattern of human response that is valid today, whatever the true nature of the demonic. This is also the case when we consider a whole different set of objections to talking about Satan. Some thinkers argue that the figure of the devil is irrelevant to the problem of evil. If the intention is to exonerate God from blame for suffering, the maneuver does not work because the question then becomes, why is the devil wicked? The appeal to a Satan figure only pushes the problem back one stage. It simply adds one more puzzle to an already perplexing picture.[11]

It may well be the case that while talk about Satan is no help in solving the problem of evil, it is important when surveying the way Jesus deals with human suffering in his day. One form of that suffering is connected in some way with some kind of figure, force, or function that is totally opposed to God's plan for the health and wholeness of God's creation. Jesus struggles mightily against that "Satan-reality" to defeat it and break its grip on humanity. Whatever its origin or nature, Satan is a force real enough to engage Jesus' attention and action. It calls forth the first assault of a fierce and costly battle Jesus wages against all that destroys or harms human beings and their life together.

CHAPTER SIX

The Miraculous Cure
of Sickness

By a count of verses, Morton Kelsy concludes that "nearly one-fifth of the entire Gospels is devoted to Jesus' healing and the discussions occasioned by it. Except for miracles in general, this is by far the greatest emphasis given to any one kind of experience in the narrative."[1] Frederick Borsch notes that in the Gospel of Mark "almost half of the narratives of Jesus' public ministry (chaps. 1-10) are devoted to Jesus' acts of power, most of which are stories of exorcism and healing."[2] Taking a larger sample, Edythe M. Daehling generously estimates that "more than half of Jesus' ministry as recorded in the Gospels was given to the healing of physical ills and restoring people to wholeness."[3] Whatever the percentage, one of the clearest evidences of God's intent to alleviate human suffering is the biblical record of miracles performed during Jesus' ministry. We now turn to this second area of God's mighty acts in overcoming evil.

Jesus' Ministry of Healing

According to the evangelist Luke, the first thing Jesus did following the temptation in the wilderness was to return to his home town and go to the synagogue. There he read these words from the book of Isaiah: "The Spirit of the Lord is upon me, because he has anointed me to preach good news to the poor. He has sent me to proclaim release to the captives and recovery of sight to the blind, to let the oppressed go free, to proclaim the year of the Lord's favor" (Luke 4:18-19). Then, according to Luke, Jesus sat down and continued, "Today this scripture has been fulfilled in your hearing (v. 21)." In this very first of Jesus' public appearances, according to Luke, Jesus made clear that his mission is to heal all manner of sickness, including the "recovery of sight to the blind."

The centrality of alleviating pain and binding up the broken in body and heart in the mission of Jesus is underscored in another incident early in his ministry. John the Baptist sent two of his disciples to Jesus to ask him, "Are you the one who is to come, or are we to wait for another?" Jesus replied, "Go and tell John what you have seen and heard: the blind receive their sight, the lame walk, the lepers are cleansed, the deaf hear, the dead are raised, the poor have good news brought to them" (Luke 7:20,22). Whatever else Jesus may have thought of himself or wanted others to think of him, he placed his healing ministry in the forefront of his "statement" of who he was. He identified himself by his acts of compassion that heal the afflicted and the needy.

By a mere count of the miracles Jesus performed, it is apparent that alleviating human distress was a top priority of his ministry. Although they are somewhat difficult to delineate, the miracles of Jesus as reported by the evangelists fall into four broad groups: nature miracles, healing miracles, raisings from the dead, and summaries of healings. Nature miracles number only seven, while there are twenty-three healing miracles and three raisings from the dead. Countless more healings are included in the ten summaries. A similar strong showing of healing miracles characterizes the list of the early church: four healing miracles and three raisings from the dead, a number equal to all the other "wonders" recorded in the Acts of the Apostles. No part of Jesus' ministry touched so many people with more significant effect than his actions of healing the sick. Along with his preaching and teaching, his miraculous cures identified him to the crowds (Mark 1:34; Luke 6:17) and, unfortunately, contributed to mounting opposition to his mission (John 11:47).

Messages in the Miracles

C. S. Lewis has written that "when pain is to be borne, a little courage helps more than much knowledge, a little human sympathy more than much courage, and the least tincture of the love of God more than all."[4] In the miracles of Jesus, we see the love of God at work to alleviate human pain. They are living enactments of God's intention and will to do away with evil. This theme is developed in a variety of directions in several of the miraculous cures at Jesus' hands.

The Man with the Withered Hand

Jesus' healing of the man with the withered hand (Mark 3:1-6) reveals that alleviating suffering was a top priority in Jesus' ministry.[5] Jesus went to the synagogue and found there a man with a withered hand. While others watched to see if Jesus would violate the sabbath law, Jesus called the man forward. Jesus asked if the law allows one to help or harm others, to save life or destroy it. The religious authorities remained silent, unwilling to give Jesus any justification for performing a cure. This display of callousness grieved and angered Jesus, who then wasted no time in healing the man's infirmity. His action broke the sabbath rule, scandalizing the onlookers and sealing his doom.

What was wrong with the Pharisees that they couldn't see the desperate need of the disabled man? Surely they were not blind nor deliberately uncaring. Mark makes it clear that the Pharisees preferred to pay attention to their religious rules rather than the insistent needs of those around them. They would not replace one iota of the law for a cup of kindness. What was most important for them was to honor the law. And the law stated there was to be no work on the sabbath, even healing the sick. Exceptions could be made in cases of life or death, but clearly a withered hand was not one of those cases. Choosing legalism over love, the Pharisees dismissed the man's appeal while condemning Jesus for his breach of tradition.

It is significant that the dogmatism of the Pharisees angers Jesus. We can understand his distress at those who desecrate the temple, and even his rebuke of dissident Peter. But is the insensitivity of the Pharisees so bad? Evidently for Jesus, to whom it was inexcusable to favor religious protocol above persons. The Pharisees were simply unable to put the needs of persons first, and Jesus was simply unable to put piety above the needs of persons.

Jesus acted to heal the disabled man because he valued health and wholeness above wooden obedience to the letter of the law. Although he did not take sabbath regulations lightly, he could not give blind allegiance to the rules where living needs were involved. With no thought for his personal safety, he chose full and abundant life in the present rather than compliance with dead regulations from the past. In doing this, Jesus suggested that God's love is active for the welfare of human beings, and that the Christian way places a high priority on alleviating suffering.

The Daughter of Jairus

Jesus' healing of the daughter of Jairus (Mark 5:21-24,35-43) likewise suggests the unshakable resolve of Jesus to alleviate suffering. While teaching by the sea, Jesus was approached by Jairus, a leader of the synagogue. Jairus pleaded with Jesus to heal his daughter. Jesus followed Jairus on his way home until they were intercepted with the news that they were too late, the girl had already died. Jesus assured the ruler that his daughter would be well, encouraged him to believe his word, and proceeded to the house.

Entering the house, Jesus startled the mourners with the announcement that the girl was not dead, but sleeping. They greeted that news with so much laughter that Jesus had to put them outside. Then, taking some disciples and the child's parents with him, Jesus went to the girl's bedside. Grasping her hand, he ordered the girl to stand up. Immediately she arose, much to the amazement of everyone there. Then Jesus commanded them to fix her something to eat.

The interesting detail in this story is Jesus' calm handling of those who laughed at him. The laughter that greeted Jesus was not the laughter that accompanies wholesome humor. It was not a supportive laughter that stated confidence in Jesus. Rather, it was a laughter *at* Jesus that said his assessment of the matter was ridiculous. Indeed, the laughter of the people was the laughter of ridicule, the laughter given to the fool. It was laughter at Jesus for his optimism, his daring to think he could do anything about the fate of the girl.

Jesus was untouched by their silly grins and sneering laughter. In contrast to the foolishness of the people, Jesus was all business. From his first word to the grieving father to his final word to the amazed parents, Jesus meant to have the girl well. Unlike the do-nothing skepticism of his scoffers, Jesus was a positive healing presence that got the job done. In the end, perhaps Jesus smiled, even laughed out loud, for joy that a life had been restored.

The story of Jairus's daughter suggests that God never laughs at those who are suffering. Rather, God's joy is in the healing of God's creation. Accordingly, Jesus could not be turned back in his mission of alleviating suffering, not even by the senseless giggles and distracting guffaws of the disbelieving. On the matter of suffering, God has the last laugh for God's love always triumphs.

The Blind Man

In spite of other interpretations, Jesus presented the healing of the blind man (John 9:1-34) as an occasion through which God's intent and action with regard to suffering is revealed. Coming upon a blind man, the disciples asked Jesus, "Rabbi, who sinned, this man or his parents, that he was born blind?" Jesus answered, "Neither this man nor his parents sinned; he was born blind so that God's works might be revealed in him."[6] Then, anointing the man's eyes with clay, Jesus instructed him to go and wash in the pool. He obeyed and returned with his sight, much to the amazement of his neighbors.

The disciples were determined to see the sickness of the man as a punishment for sin. In that approach to the situation, they were reflecting the attitude of the Pharisees. The Pharisees seemed obsessed with sniffing out sin wherever they went. They accused the blind man and Jesus of being sinners, and so intimidated the man's parents that they wouldn't even protect their son's welfare.

Jesus didn't accept the argument that sickness was due to sin. To be sure, there are some cures where sin did seem to be a factor, but here it is not. Rather—and this is the significant maneuver—Jesus pointed the attention of his disciples in another direction, "that the works of God might be made manifest in him." Jesus wasn't so much interested in the moral record of the man as in making the occasion a positive statement of God's love and power. Jesus didn't even require that the man have faith! The man's faith didn't enter the picture until *after* the cure. How different from the popular religious thought of the day.

Furthermore, Jesus didn't hesitate one minute in curing the man's blindness. Jesus did not stop to debate the theological subtleties in the situation or the anticipated cure. He merely stated his judgment on the matter, and then proceeded with the healing. Rather than wrestle with the intellectual problem of why there is suffering, Jesus acted to overcome the suffering. Quickly dismissing the Pharisees' "solution," Jesus offered his own treatment: "Go to Siloam and wash."

This miracle at Jesus' hand illustrates the love of a God who acts to restore sight to the blind. While his disciples want to discuss the theological implications of the sickness, Jesus proceeds to rid the man of its curse. To clinch the point, Jesus explicitly declares that the love and power of God's *overcoming* this malady is exactly what the sickness *means*. Jesus denies the man's blindness any right to exist or carry importance other than as an occasion to declare God's will and strength in overcoming suffering.

The Epileptic Boy

The divine resolve to help and heal broken human lives and bodies is impressively documented in Jesus' cure of the epileptic boy (Mark 9:14-29). A concerned father brought his stricken son to the disciples, who were unable to cure him. Jesus arrived on the scene and was told of the failure of his followers. Jesus reprimanded the disciples, and ordered the boy brought to him. After describing the boy's medical history, the father pleaded with Jesus to heal his son. Jesus replied, "All things can be done for the one who believes." Immediately the father responded with these painfully honest words, "I believe; help my unbelief!" With that confession made, a crowd began to gather, and Jesus took action to heal the epileptic boy. Convulsions left the boy limp and lifeless. Finally, Jesus took him by the hand and raised him, cured, composed, and very much alive.

The role of faith in this miracle is complex. For lack of faith, says Matthew (17:19-21), the disciples were unable to cure the epileptic boy. Jesus clearly stated that it is faith that makes all things possible. It is hard to imagine higher accolades for faith than are given in this story.

On the other hand, the plaintive plea of the father, "I believe; help my unbelief," suggests that a strong, unalloyed faith is not necessary for a person to receive God's blessing. The faith of the father was a mixture of belief and unbelief. It is as though he was convinced of the good intentions of Jesus, but was not sure that Jesus had the capability to perform this miracle. Perhaps the father had tried other cures that had failed. Surely, the inability of the disciples to heal the boy must have weighed on his mind at that point. It would have been reasonable to harbor some doubt about the success of any attempted cure of his son.

Nevertheless, it is not the father but Jesus who is at the center of this miracle. He moved decisively to cure the boy in the midst of the ambiguous faith of the father. Whatever the man lacked in faith, Jesus made up in compassion. Faith may have helped save others. In this miracle, however, it was Jesus' mercy that effected the cure, regardless of the faith present.

Perhaps Jesus sensed the struggle of the father to want to believe that a cure for his son was possible. Perhaps out of sympathy for the father's wrestling with his doubts, Jesus blessed the boy and the man. It is also possible that this is a story about God's single-minded intent to help those in distress. The father was determined to see his son well again, even though he had little within himself to commend a cure. The Father in heaven is also singularly concerned with healing a hurting creation, even though the faith of those sufferers may be mixed with unbelief.

The focus of this miracle is not so much the faith and lack of faith of the father, as poignant as that may be, as it is the love of God in relation to that man's agnosticism. The shadows in that struggle serve to set in even more brightness the brilliance of God's work in alleviating suffering. God's healing work is greater than any obstacles we might set before it. The divine caretaking will not be slowed, not even by those of uncertain faith. Although we may be weak in faith, God is strong in reserves of compassion and the capability to help the afflicted.

Blind Bartimaeus

The greatest hindrance to an appreciation of the intent and power of God to overcome suffering is doubt. Doubt is the great destroyer. It is the white flag of defeat, the blackness that holds out the dawn, the pall that shuts out hope. Doubt rises within us to smother our determination to believe God is great and God is good. Because events may not turn out the way we would like as soon as we would like, doubt rises within us. The story of blind Bartimaeus (Mark 10:46-52) invites us to struggle against doubt, and to believe that God will come to our rescue sooner or later. It pictures the kind of tough faith that holds on to God until God heals.

Sitting by the roadside, Bartimaeus heard Jesus pass by. He called, "Jesus, Son of David, have mercy on me!" Jesus heard his plea and invited him to come closer. He approached Jesus, who asked him what he wanted. "My teacher, let me see again," he pleaded. Commending his faith, Jesus healed his blindness. Delivered of his handicap, Bartimaeus followed Jesus, praising God.

We do not know exactly how long Bartimaeus had been blind. Perhaps it was from birth. In any case, he probably had good reason to have given up hope for a cure. Yet he perceived in Jesus the possibility of a miracle. He understood that it was the intent and ministry of Jesus to heal the sick and eliminate suffering of any sort. This vision fueled his faith and gave him the strength to pursue Jesus until he received a cure.

This perseverance survived even the rebukes of the onlookers who, according to the other synoptic writers, commanded him to be silent. Even when he reached Jesus, he was met with a puzzling question that required that he verbalize his request. Bartimaeus's unflinching certainty that God means us well is like the attitude of Job in the Old Testament and the Syrophoenician woman in the New. It also reminds us of Jesus' parable of the widow and the lawyer, with its admonition never to let up on our prayers to God.

We may want to believe that God cares, but extended suffering may cloud our resolve. Doubt may plague our soul, rebuking our faith and taunting us to give up our confidence in God. The story of Bartimaeus is an encouragement to us never to give up our trust in God's intent and ability to make us well. It is a plea to us to stand tall no matter how much we are buffeted. And it is a word of assurance that God will deliver. Eventually, the God who desires the well-being of all he has made will restore and uphold us in victory and peace.

The Infirm Man

The miracles illustrate that God not only is sufficient to the task of curing sickness, but also will work as long as necessary to overcome evil. This perseverance is suggested especially by Jesus' healing of the infirm man (John 5:1-9). One day, Jesus noticed a man who was unable to make his way to the healing waters at the Bethzatha pool. Instructing him to rise, pick up his bed, and walk, Jesus cured the man on the spot. However, because the miracle occurred on the sabbath, and the man carried his bed on the sabbath, both Jesus and the healed man were condemned by the religious authorities.

The Pharisees objected to Jesus healing on the sabbath because it violated the sabbath law. They defended the sabbath law with the teaching that God created the world in six days and rested on the sabbath. Therefore, they reasoned, everyone else should complete their labors in six days and remain idle on the sabbath. Only in dire emergencies was any work or health care allowed.

Apparently that was the wrong tactic to take with Jesus. We have already noted how Jesus paid little attention to the sabbath law when human welfare was at stake. More profound, he seems to have rejected the general notion that God's work ended on the sixth day of creation, saying, "My Father is still working, and I also am working" (John 5:17). For Jesus, God was not a distant clock maker who got the world going and then retired. Rather, God was a continuously present power, creating and sustaining throughout all time, right down to the present. Jesus apparently regarded his own healing power as an extension of that divine, ever-present creativity. He was the living sign that the Father's work had not ended, but was still wresting order out of chaos in the generations long after the creation.

Jesus made the creative power of God a real force in his day. He gathered that power into his command to the sea, "Be still," his word to the sick, "Arise," and every life-restoring action of his ministry. Over the powers of darkness he had the last word: "See, you are well." In him God's work of creating and making whole broke out again and again to heal, restore, and comfort the creation.

Most important, Jesus revealed that God is working still to embrace all things in the divine everlasting arms. Today there are still many who think that God's involvement with the world ended at creation. Doubting God's power to help those who are suffering today, they lock God in a box stored among the ancient artifacts of history. That box should not be opened, so they reason, because God's part in this creation is sealed in the past. We should leave God alone and make our own way in the world, including the world of pain and sorrow.

That kind of thinking is shattered by Jesus' words in this miracle. Jesus proclaims that God is not locked up in the past, but is a real factor in every age. God moves in the elements and galaxies of the universe. God is present in DNA and fills the smallest cell. God shapes the human will and watches over the course of history. And, yes, God is working to help us subdue the terrors and despair that accompany sickness, and to turn back suffering itself, just as Jesus did in his day. This is the vision that Christ would share with us: "My Father is still working, and I also am working."

Issues Addressed by Jesus' Ministry of Healing

The prominence of miracles of healing in Jesus' ministry speaks to several issues that often surface in discussions of the intellectual problem of evil, including the relationship of sickness and sin, the will of God, and the possibility of miracles in our own day.

Sickness and Sin

A young woman suffering from a disease that causes gradual organ deterioration came to me one day to report that a second eye exam had disclosed another tumor, this one lodged in her remaining good eye. Already having endured the loss of one lung, brain surgery, and a host of physical ailments, this woman was tormented by doubts about her complicity in her misfortune. "I don't know what is wrong with my life," she despaired. "What am I doing to make this happen to me?"

Oftentimes illness will elicit feelings of guilt. Suffering causes people to review their lives, looking for places where they might have gone wrong or erred in judgment. The linking of sickness and sin was commonplace in biblical times. The friends of Job were sure his misfortune was the result of sin. The Pharisees in Jesus' day made the same identification of sin as the cause of sickness (John 9:2).

Clearly there is a tradition within Scripture that does link sin and suffering. According to the prophets, it was because of their waywardness that the Israelites were oppressed by foreign invaders (Amos 3:11; Isa. 9:11; Hos. 10:10). The wisdom literature of the Old Testament, including Psalms and Proverbs, praises the good health of the righteous, and notes the trials of the wicked (Ps. 1). The whole legalistic system of emerging Judaism rested on a scheme of rewards and punishments for moral behavior (Deut. 11:16-17).

This rationale is also reflected in the New Testament, where Jesus identifies sin as the reason for physical impairment (John 5:14; Mark 2:5). On the other hand, there are many instances where it is not clear just what role the suffering person's behavior has played in his or her distress (Luke 17:11-19; Mark 7:31-37). There are also occasions recorded where suffering is clearly disassociated from sin (Luke 13:2-5; John 9:3).

In the story of the miraculous cure of the blind man discussed above, the concern of Jesus is not with the matter of punishment for guilt. Jesus moved quickly to cure the man's blindness.[7] That action, as well as the action of all other cures at the hands of the Great Physician, is the new Word of God on the issue of sin and sickness. Jesus' ministry of healing is the exclamation point on the divine intention to rid the world of evil. It is Jesus' campaign against suffering that is the new focus of the gospel. The question, "Who sinned?" is simply a distraction in the face of the enormous spiritual energy available in Jesus, energy that is directed to one purpose, namely, to alleviate human suffering.

Was It God's Will?

There are few experiences in life that cause people to think more about God and God's involvement in the world than the experience of suffering. Suffering reveals that human nature is theologically fickle. While we may be quite reserved about crediting good fortune to divine intervention, we are much more ready to implicate God in our misfortune. It is for this reason that Stephen Wold makes good sense when he writes, "Confusion about God's will is a subject that calls for clear thinking in a world that is filled with suffering and pain."[8]

In reflecting on her paralysis sustained in a diving accident, Joni Eareckson writes, "God has placed each of us exactly where He pleases on the scale of suffering."[9] Attributing evil to God's will and then looking for some good in it is one way to explain human suffering. When terrible tragedy strikes, we grasp for some meaning, some sense to the events before our eyes. Some people are willing to go so far as to say, "God planned this accident," in order to restore order to the world. Such a statement is assurance that God is still in control of the world and that all is well, even in the midst of tragic suffering.[10]

We have seen that the biblical record pictures a God of justice whose righteousness sometimes explodes in wrath. We can find biblical texts (such as Exod. 4:11, Lam. 3:38, and Isa. 45:7) that suggest that God sends suffering to the people.[11] There is a developed tradition that says God deals with the moral evil of the world by sending judgment.[12] All these approaches implicate God in at least some of the suffering that goes on in the world.

However, it must be noted that the suffering that God allegedly sends is always part of a larger struggle against moral evil, a struggle that occurs for the ultimate benefit of humankind. The harsh hand of God's discipline is always applied as an act of divine love. While this can sometimes cause perplexing reflections, it may be the only way that a sturdy faith can develop, a faith that trusts in God in spite of seemingly excessive divine correction. Joni writes, "Where does God get the nerve to claim that He lets me break my neck because he loves me so much? Some kind of love!"[13] But she also believes God filters suffering "through fingers of love, giving us only that which works for good and which He knows will point us to Him."[14]

More important, the kind of thinking that attributes suffering to God's will must not be allowed to prevail without noting the considerable evidence to the contrary. For every time that Scripture implicates God in human suffering, there are several stories that show God rescuing people from suffering. While we cannot settle the matter by counting stories, we can certainly argue that any claim that God sends suffering to people must be qualified by "the rest of the story." Yes, some suffering seems to result from the way people lead lives contrary to God's will, but this does not make God a callous or sadistic God. To the contrary, the record of Scripture, and especially Jesus' healing miracles, portray a God largely engaged in alleviating suffering, a God whose heart feels deeply the pains of the people and whose hands reach out to rescue them from suffering.

Miracles Today?

The stories of Jesus' miraculous healings seem to many like fantasies from a distant past. Yet if God is the same yesterday, today, and tomorrow, it would seem possible that miracles could occur today. If God through Jesus performed miracles in ancient times, and God is still God today, then it seems logical that miracles could cure people in modern times. Joe Stevenson believes such a miracle occurred in the healing of his terminally ill son.[15] And Brian Sternberg still awaits a miracle to cure his paralysis caused by an accident in 1963. Sternberg's parents exhibit a steely faith in God's will to heal:

> The Jesus we saw in the Bible came to bring healing. Where there was hurt, He touched and made well. He never cursed or afflicted people. Jesus was God's language to man. What God is, Jesus lived. Has God's language changed? . . . I don't think God is very happy with Brian's condition either. God's will as seen in the Bible is a full, abundant life. It's wholeness, health — not the body Brian's trapped in.[16]

The hope that God will miraculously cure sickness today is not shared by all Christians. For some, like Joni Eareckson, their chastened outlook has been learned the hard way. Convinced that God would cure her, Joni attended healing services, but to no avail. While she continued to believe in miracles, she concluded that God does not heal all people, but allows suffering for the benefits it can bring.[17] A similar stand is taken by Philip Yancey, who distinguishes his approach from that of Brian Sternberg and his family. Yancey favors the position that God does not need to heal everyone, but allows some pain for the benefits it brings. While God may sometimes intervene, for the most part it is up to us to bear one another's burdens.[18] These more reserved estimates of the likelihood of miracles occurring today are somewhat supported by the qualifications imposed by Jesus in the early church. On more than one occasion, Jesus acted and spoke in a way that undercut popular interest in "signs" (Mark 8:12; John 4:48; Luke 10:17-20), and Paul wrote that while some look for signs, "we proclaim Christ crucified" (1 Cor. 1:23).

However, it may be that the skeptic is too cautious in ruling out the possibility of miracles occurring today. David Hume denied the possibility of miracles on the grounds that they are contrary to natural law and are supported by unreliable witnesses.[19] However, it seems Hume overstated the authority of natural law, and understated the reliability of testimony to miracles. On the first account, Hume failed to recognize that natural laws are only statistical statements, and that they therefore allow for unusual anomalies to occur. In fact, Joseph Fichter reports testimony to an astonishing number of miracles in religious hospital settings. In one study, an astounding thirty-eight percent of the personnel at a church-related institution said a miraculous remission had occurred in their hospital, and almost two-thirds of those could even describe the miracle![20] As for Hume's judgment that witnesses to miracles are too few in numbers and are unreliable, there seem to be cases where miracles are observed by many witnesses who appear to have their wits about them. The miracles at Lourdes, for instance, seem to meet standards of scientific verification for even their harshest critics. They are attested by many witnesses who are educated, have good judgment, and are not given to sensationalism.[21]

While denying that the possibility of miraculous healings may be a case of "underbelief" in view of biblical and contemporary experience, the greatest importance of miracles today is as a type of approach to the problem of suffering. Miraculous cures of sickness make a statement about God's will and human responsibility in the face of suffering. C. S. Lewis has said that a miracle is a natural process accelerated, an occasion when God "speeds up" the regular support and direction that God always supplies the world.[22] The implication of that view is that "seeds" of miracles are present in the ordinary course of events. Actions expended to alleviate suffering are a miracle of God's supportive care carried out on the human level and at a natural pace. When people work to reduce the volume of suffering in the world, their compassionate caring is a mini-miracle in the order of things, a micro-instance of God's grand scheme of healing and redemption.

The occurrence of miracles in biblical and contemporary times is not a discouragement but an encouragement to an activist theodicy. Miracles do not compete with human initiatives in reducing suffering, but point to the importance of that action in reducing suffering. As miracles are God's dramatic way of dealing with pain and infirmity, so healing and helping ministries are the way human beings deal with the same problems. Indeed, wherever such caring assistance is extended, a kind of miracle takes place, the miracle of lives changed from egocentricity to concern for others. A form of incarnation takes place as God's love finds human shape. A prefiguring of resurrection occurs as persons are born again as compassionate caregivers. Where the hungry are given adequate supply, the sick are healed by medicine, and the despairing are given hope, there miracles occur as surely as when Jesus fed the multitudes, cured the lame, and preached good news to the captives.

CHAPTER SEVEN

Overcoming the Last Enemy

A little boy writes:

Dear God,

> What is it like when you die.
> Nobody will tell me. I just want to know,
> I don't want to do it.
>
> >Your friend
> >Mike.[1]

For most people, the wish to avoid death probably grows in direct proportion to their proximity to it. The older we become and the closer to death we move, the more we "don't want to do it." Hans Küng expressed well the normal human aversion to death: "Even when we die late, we still die too early."[2]

While tough-minded thinkers can muster up some supposedly good reasons for death—the corrective for old age, the process of making room for the next generation, protection against possible further sins or mistakes—their arguments convince few people, if any. Death remains the most-traveled highway, around which everyone would like to detour.

Even for Christian faith, death is an "enemy" to be defeated (1 Cor. 15:24-26). At the least it is an unpleasantness most people would like to escape. Woody Allen voices that sentiment when he quips, "It's not that I'm afraid to die. I just don't want to be there when it happens." Nor do we care to spend eternity in its company. On her seventy-fifth birthday, Margaret Mead announced, that although she would die someday, she would not retire. If we can't avoid death, we would like to remove its sting, at least.

Why is death so fearsome, and what is the Christian response to it? Let us turn next to a consideration of the suffering that death imposes on the human condition, and the triumph over the terror of death that Christianity promises.

Death is Evil

Although the death rate is the same in every generation, namely, one death per person, it is alarming news when we apply it to ourselves. It is one statistic we wish we could escape. On this point, we don't want to be counted with the rest. The prospect of death sweeping us away with millions of others, leaving only a cold number for our legacy, chills our hearts. We cringe before the terrifying inevitability, the awful impersonality of it all. In the face of our inescapable demise, life becomes a living hell, our souls "tormented by the little death knells of ticktocking time, and haunted even more by the silences of eternity."[3]

Death is the ultimate insult. It is the final affront that yields no compromise. In death we come to our personal end. Death is the black horseman who skewers us on his unforgiving lance. We stand for the battle with nowhere to turn. We raise our defenses with no hope of protection. The shrouded ghost advances with flashing sword and cuts us down, scattering our bodies, spilling our blood, draining our lives. This thinking, feeling, loving, creating, hoping person that is me ceases to exist, is no more, swept from the face of the earth, never to return. Death has dealt the final blow, from which there is no recovery.

Death is the terrifying dissolution of our very selves. It is the victory of nonbeing over being. It is the body of Mozart thrown into a pauper's grave, clothed in a burlap sack. A shovelful of lime anoints the remains, not to hallow or preserve them, but to disinfect and decompose them. The exquisite organization of the human being collapses into silent dust. Nothing is left but the relentless process of returning to the elements from which our bodies were made.

We watch the television, unable to turn away as the *Challenger* shuttle blows up in a flaming explosion. We catch our breath, try to comprehend what we see, then turn to another channel for another view of the disaster. We can hardly believe our eyes. We want to be sure about what we see. We are also transfixed by the horror of it all. Something within us resonates with the awful drama that we see. Isn't this what we fear in our inmost being will happen to ourselves? To be blown apart, to disintegrate without trace, is the maximal terror. In one instant, the shuttle disaster showed us the face of death in its worst mask. This is precisely what death is, no matter what form it takes. Death is the final assault on our personal being. At death we are unhinged, dismembered, scattered to the winds. Death begins the process by which we slowly come apart, collapse without trace, vanish from the face of the earth. We are utterly gone, without a remembrance that we were ever here.

We recoil before the absurdity of death. Paul Goodman wrote a book, *Growing Up Absurd*, about the insanities we encounter living in the modern world. Actually, death is much more absurd than life, as crazy as that can be. In spite of all the emptiness and folly in life, death is far more pathetic. While we live, we can struggle to eke out a meaning for our existence. We can find little islands of sanity in the vast sea of absurdity around us. But death simply cancels all possibilities for anything like that continuing on. It brings our little victories to an abrupt and absolute end. And in doing that, death ravages even those minitriumphs. If our life is to come to nothing in the end, then what is the value of anything we accomplish or experience along the way? If nothing has lasting value, does it have any value at all? What sense is there to our struggles if death triumphs ultimately? If we are here merely to die, what is the point of it all? Why bother? Death is the consummate robber, stealing all meaning from life.

The Christian Testimony to Victory Over the Grave

In the midst of all the darkness of death, Christianity lifts a beacon of hope. Nothing can separate us from the love of God, not even death. If death is a mighty power over life, God is mightier still. The Christian drama pictures the power of God at work overcoming the power of death. While there are some intimations of eternal life in the Old Testament (Isa. 25:8; Dan. 12:2), the prime actor in this drama is Jesus Christ, who in words and deeds declares an end to the tyranny of death.

Jesus shared with his followers the vision of an eternal kingdom of God where those who suffered for their discipleship will be rewarded. Jesus said to them:

Truly I tell you, at the renewal of all things, when the Son of Man is seated on the throne of his glory, you who have followed me will also sit on twelve thrones, judging the twelve tribes of Israel. And everyone who has left houses or brothers or sisters or father or mother or children or fields, for my name's sake, will receive a hundredfold, and will inherit eternal life. (Matt. 19:28-29)

The first Christians looked forward to "new heavens and a new earth, where righteousness is at home" (2 Pet. 3:13). They anticipated the "revealing of the children of God," when they would enjoy "adoption, the redemption of our bodies" (Rom. 8:19,23). They were comforted under persecution by the promise of Jesus that God had a place for them in heaven, and that he, Jesus, was going ahead to ready that place for them (John 14:2-3). Even as he faced the death of a martyr, Stephen "gazed into heaven and saw the glory of God and Jesus standing at the right hand of God" (Acts 7:55).

Jesus devoted a significant portion of his healing ministry to raising the dead. A funeral procession was passing by one day, carrying the body of a young boy, the only son of a widow. Moved with compassion, Jesus approached the bier and restored the man to life (Luke 7:11-17). Another day, while teaching, Jesus was approached on behalf of a ruler's daughter. Jesus proceeded to her side and, amidst much wailing and jeering, commanded her to arise (Luke 8:49-56). Yet another time, a dear friend of Jesus, Lazarus, died and had been buried. Jesus went to his tomb, commanded the stone be removed, and called to Lazarus to come out. Still bandaged and wrapped in cloth, the dead man, now restored, emerged from the grave (John 11:38-44). In all these dramatic encounters, Jesus made clear his intention to deal with death by overcoming it.

This intention was no more evident than in his own death and resurrection. Jesus repeatedly informed his followers that his life would soon end, but that he would be raised again from the dead (Matt. 16:21, 17:22-23, 20:17-19). He spoke of a future day when the Son of Man, presumably himself, seated at the right hand of power, would come on the clouds of heaven (Mark 14:62; Matt. 26:64; Luke 22:69). Following his death on the cross, he escaped the tomb (Matt. 28:1-7; Mark 16:1-8; Luke 24:1-9; John 20:11-18), and appeared as the risen Lord to many people (Matt. 28:9-10; Luke 24:13-31; 1 Cor. 15:3-9). It was the certain conviction of the early church that Jesus "abolished death and brought life and immortality to light" (2 Tim. 1:10), and, as a mighty warrior against the Dark Prince, was able to "destroy the one who has the power of death, that is, the devil" (Heb. 2:14).

Not only did the church believe Jesus had overcome death, it made that belief the pivotal confession in the faith. Of all the parts of the message, the part about Jesus' resurrection was the least expendable. Virtually everything depended on that victory: "If Christ has not been raised, then our proclamation has been in vain and your faith has been in vain. . . . If Christ has not been raised, your faith is futile and you are still in your sins" (1 Cor. 15:14,17). Jesus' defeat of death was the foremost message of the apostles who "gave their testimony to the resurrection of the Lord Jesus" (Acts 4:33). The early Christians described themselves as a people called to a hope based on "the immeasurable greatness of [God's] power for us who believe, according to the working of his great power. God put this power to work in Christ when he raised him from the dead and seated him at his right hand in the heavenly places" (Eph. 1:19-20). The resurrection of Jesus was the Christian's strength and stay. It was the premier exhibit in the believer's case for taking up the faith.

Jesus' victory over death was also the foremost evidence in the believer's claim that Christianity deals with suffering by overcoming it. The pioneer church made this point convincingly by assuring all the followers of Jesus a victory similar to his own (1 Pet. 1:3-4). Jesus promised eternal life to those who believe in him (John 3:36, 5:24, 6:47, 20:31). His own victory would be passed on to the faithful (John 5:21, 11:25, 14:19). The first Christians picked up on this promise and preached that as God raised up Jesus from the dead so God will raise up his faithful (1 Cor. 6:14; 2 Cor. 4:14). Christ is the "first fruits" of the new life, through whom "all will be made alive" (1 Cor. 15:20-22). He is the keeper of the keys of heaven who will refashion his children for life eternal: "But our citizenship is in heaven, and it is from there that we are expecting a Savior, the Lord Jesus Christ. He will transform the body of our humiliation that it may be conformed to the body of his glory, by the power that enables him to make all things subject to himself" (Phil. 3:20-21; see also Rom. 8:10-11).

Most significant for a discussion of the problem of evil, eternal life marks the victory of God over human suffering. Life everlasting is the quintessential word in the biblical message on the problem of evil. It is the time when those who have sacrificed on earth will be rewarded in heaven (Mark 10:29-30), the persecuted will be blessed (Matt. 5:10-11), and those who wept in pain will find joy (John 16:20-21). In heaven the redeemed will sit at table with God (Matt. 8:11; Luke 13:29) and dwell securely in God's mansion (John 14:2). "They will hunger no more, and thirst no more; the sun will not strike them, nor any scorching heat; for the Lamb at the center of the throne will be their shepherd, and he will guide them to springs of the water of life, and God will wipe away every tear from their eyes" (Rev. 7:16-17; see also 21:3-4).

Issues of Eternal Life
Is It Realistic?

Is it realistic to look to eternal life when facing the problem of evil? Because of the excesses sometimes associated with the notion of heaven, critics have discredited the idea. Steve Martin drew from the popular characterization of heaven when he asked, "Wouldn't it be weird if you died and you woke up and you were in Heaven—just like they always told you? . . . And everybody had wings and harps and there were pearly gates . . . Wouldn't you feel stupid?"[4] From a more serious perspective, C. S. Lewis wrote, "All that stuff about family reunions 'on the further shore,' pictured in entirely earthly terms . . . is all unscriptural, all out of bad hymns and lithographs. There's not a word of it in the Bible. And it rings false. We *know* it couldn't be like that. Reality never repeats."[5] Yet for others, heaven is the last hope for a just and happy life. Only the cruel and callous would deny Joni Eareckson her dream of a heaven where she will trade in her paralyzed body for a new one, healed and whole.[6]

In fact, there are many serious thinkers for whom the only or at least the central solution to the problem of evil lies in eternal life, or God's coming kingdom, whichever arrives first. Nels Ferré believes that there is no other viable solution to the problem of evil than life everlasting.[7] William Fitch also maintains that the future triumph of God in the eschatological kingdom is the only thing that can vindicate Christian faith.[8] John Hick proposes an eschatological resolution as the ultimate answer to the problem of evil.[9] Brian Hebblethwaite argues that the absolute good of a future perfected creation will justify the evil that presently exists.[10] J. Christiaan Beker proposes that Paul's answer of a future victory over evil is to be preferred to the picture in Luke-Acts of God's providence within and use of suffering.[11] Clearly, the idea of a future vindication of the suffering people undergo in this life is a viable proposal among theodicists today.

Whatever the merit of that proposal as an argument for justifying faith in God, our interest is primarily in the message that the hope of heaven conveys to those who suffer about God's dealings with suffering. That message is that God wishes to have suffering over and done with. The promise of life eternal is a declaration of the Christian view that evil has no ultimate lodging in God's kingdom. Evil is an imposter with no rights, an alien with no citizenship papers, a foreigner with no home in the city of God. If this is not perfectly clear in this earthly life, it will be clear in the life to come. The ultimate demise of suffering, a kingdom where there is no more pain or tears, is the real world of which this present life is only a dim anticipation.

Is It Reasonable?

But is it reasonable to look at the world in that way? John Hick observes, "In our contemporary Western scientific culture, most people (including most members of the various Churches) find it almost impossible to take seriously the thought of a life after death."[12] One of the reasons that the notion of life after death is not seriously entertained by our modern, learned culture is that such a notion cannot possibly deliver what it promises. The hope of heaven is hope in the survival of the earthly or predeath person. But it is obvious that a critical part of that person does not survive, namely, the body and its brain. Karl Barth wryly observes, "Some day we shall be buried. Some day a company of men will process out to a churchyard and lower a coffin and everyone will go home; but one will not come back, and that will be me."[13] However much our popular culture may deny it, death claims each and every one of us, in each and every part of our being.

How is it possible, then, the objection goes, for life to resume after death? If it is the case that "without my body, I am nobody at all,"[14] how can a person be the same person after death as before? It is simply not enough for a soul or mind or memory to survive. A disembodied person is only a ghost of the self! Nor is it sufficient that the person be outfitted with a new body, for that also would mean a new identity. If people are not "gap-inclusive"—that is, able to leap over the gap from death to eternal life while maintaining their identity—then there can be no "life" after death in any meaningful way.[15]

This objection to eternal life is well reasoned but religiously inappropriate. Of all the times when rationality ought to yield to faith, this is foremost. Death is the ultimate surrender of our life, the end of all our powers, including our rational powers. Death is the introduction of radical new possibilities. Teilhard de Chardin writes that at death we literally come apart so that God can enter the very cells of our being.[16] Death is a new order where those things thought impossible by us become realities through God's power. Paul seems to have had this transformation in mind when he spoke in defense of life after death, "Why is it thought incredible by any of you that God raises the dead?" (Acts 26:8).

It might be farfetched to think that we have something within us that is gap-inclusive. It might be unrealistic to think that human philosophy could prove the existence of immortality or that cryogenics could fool death. But why is it thought incredible that *God* could raise the dead? Isn't that just what we mean when we think of God? Isn't God just the kind of agent who could bring off a resurrection, if anyone could? Surely, that is the point of view of the New Testament, where Jesus' resurrection is clearly the work of God (Acts 2:24; Rom. 6:4, 8:11; 1 Cor. 6:14; 2 Cor. 4:14; Heb. 13:20; 1 Pet. 1:21). Luther made the point that resurrection is no big deal to a God who can make the world and so many other things including saints, *out of nothing*![17] If God flings the planets to their places and weaves life into the strands of DNA, surely God has the power to preserve our identity in a life after death. Though it may not be obvious to us just how God does it, in the light of faith it is clear that one can reasonably believe that it is possible.[18]

Can It Compensate?

Finally, even if Christianity proclaims a future victory over death through the resurrection of Jesus Christ, is that enough to compensate for past suffering? Frederick Sontag doubts that any future heavenly existence could justify the amount of evil in the present.[19] John Roth wonders about the "millions who have suffered without justification and died without peace."[20] No amount of heavenly bliss, so the objection goes, can outweigh the accumulation of murdered, violated, broken, and defeated humanity.[21] One tough-minded critic has vowed that if he gets to heaven he will thank God for entrance to such nice surroundings, but still ask the Almighty why God chose the way God did on earth.[22]

It would be inhumane and callous to deny the awful suffering that darkens the pages of history—the bubonic plague, the Lisbon earthquake, the Holocaust, and Hiroshima. Nothing can be done to change that record of catastrophic evil and enormous suffering. However, it is possible that the past record can be cast in a new light.[23] Jesus' story of the woman who forgets the pain of childbirth for joy that a new life has been born into the world is a case in point (John 16:21). Paul said that our present sufferings are not worth comparing with the glory that is to be revealed (Rom. 8:18). Also, what God has prepared for those who believe is simply beyond comprehension (1 Cor. 2:9). The plea of the Christian is that the future kingdom of righteousness and joy be included in the picture when weighing the amount of good and evil in the world. No one knows enough to be a pessimist, to say categorically, for instance, that the future won't tip the scales in favor of a just and good world.[24]

The debate over the validity of the eschatological argument that God will make it all right at the end of time does not undermine the value of the Christian claim that God deals with death by doing battle against it and defeating it. In fact, one participant in the debate, John Roth, has proposed an activist response to the eschatological argument. He suggests that the way to increase the balance of good over evil is by eliminating human suffering.[25] Apart from its use for building a theodicy, an active overcoming of evil by citizens and caregivers is the strategy of choice for the Christian. The struggle of Jesus with the last enemy and the vision of Easter are the ultimate expressions of that strategy.

A "Final" Word

Of all the evils that human beings must endure, death is the most resistant to attack. Like the ancient philosopher Epicurus, we can try mightily to talk our way out of the problem: "Death cannot get hold of me, because when I am, death is not, and when death is, I am not." However, our clever rhetoric cannot save us. Like so many efforts to logically wriggle free from the sentence of death, this little piece of reasoning collapses. Its fatal flaw is its second term, "when death is, I am not." If there is a time when I am not, then death has won the battle. We do not escape death by not being. The situation of not being is another way to describe death.

As scornful as death is to verbal attack, Christian faith is unyielding in its trust in God to win the final battle. The suffering of the believer is a hopeful suffering,[26] anchored in the biblical testimony to resurrection. Whatever evils may come, the Christian clings to that anchor. Indeed, it is that anchor that holds faith steady in the midst of the worst storms of life. It is the hope of heaven that protects faith from despair in this life. The believer is confident that God will help him or her in real, practical ways. The hope of heaven secures that confidence in spite of awful suffering in this life.

Although believers may not be certain of the next step in their pilgrimage, they are certain of the final step. This allows faith to take whatever comes its way and still survive. Faith makes continuous adjustments to reality in order to preserve its own integrity. If pain persists, if suffering grows, if death draws near, the belief that God will help is progressively refined until it means that God will help by raising the suffering person to eternal life. There is a stubbornness about faith that rests finally with its hope of heaven. No matter how insistent suffering is, faith is equally resilient. Its vision is locked on an ultimate overcoming of evil as the real and final word of God on human suffering.

PART THREE

PART THREE

Ingredients in Carevision

CHAPTER EIGHT

Caregiving As Vocation

In the chapters of Part 2 we reviewed the biblical testimony to God's action in overcoming evil. While this testimony is at the center of carevision, it is not the sum of that response. To focus only on the biblical record of God's mighty acts in overcoming evil without connecting that story to any human follow-up is to tell only half of the story. In fact, it is to rob the ancient story of any meaning for the present. As John Roth has noted, the triumph of Jesus over the world is credible only if people today embody his compassionate way by living for others.[1]

To tell the ancient story without relating it to the present world is also to deny the present any "lessons" from the past and to deny God any role in human affairs except in the past. It is to overlook the fact that God "is with all human beings everywhere, working incessantly to check the forces of destruction, to heal those who are injured, and to coax into full activity those energies which have been blocked."[2] We would add that God is active not only everywhere, but in every time, and especially now through others who follow God's way. This point is particularly relevant when dealing with the issue of God's role in suffering.

It is important, then, to suggest just how the biblical message might be developed in the world today. To outline a plan for Christian care today is, in effect, to propose the actions that comprise the "arguments" in carevision, to encourage the deeds of mercy that make up the caring part of carevision. Such a plan would suggest the vast scope of actions that can apply to the problem of evil.

In this part, therefore, we will first explore some basic matters: how caregiving is a dynamic built into creation itself, how the Christian is also called to an intensive vocation of self-spending caregiving, and how, through God's grace and human faith, this call can be answered. Caregiving is founded on an awareness of God's prior care of us and a commitment to become co-creators with God in caring for this creation. We will then briefly look at four areas where caregiving can function: the ecological order, the social order, the intellectual order, and the personal order. These areas represent both the challenge and the opportunity to develop carevision over a wide variety of situations.

The Pastoral Order Throughout Creation

On Sunday, March 13, 1988, an electrical spark ignited a fire on a tree-covered mountain of Shimian County in Sichuan province in China. Located near an oil depot, the fire threatened lives and homes in the nearby county town. Lai Ning, a fourteen-year-old boy, had just left his house for a walk when he saw the smoke in the distance. Running to the site, he met two classmates also attracted by the fire. Together they fought the fire until dusk when authorities ordered everyone away. As they were being driven from the charred hillside, they jumped out of the back of the truck and returned to the fire. They continued to beat back the flames all night until the fire was extinguished. Two of the boys returned home, but Lai Ning was missing. A search was organized, and at nine o'clock the next morning the boy's crumpled body was found. In a futile effort to escape the fire, he had dragged himself along the ground until finally overcome. In his hand was a pine branch he had used to beat out the fire.[3]

Although the story of Lai Ning has become embellished with legend and distorted by politics, the fundamental action of the boy putting out the fire has never been disputed. It is a poignant tale of dedication and sacrifice that illustrates the fact that effort to overcome danger and suffering is a universal human value, not one just of Christian, Western cultures. Whether applied to the preservation of nature or the preservation of human life, taking action to turn back destruction seems to be an inherent law of humanity. Although it is sometimes submerged beneath the enraged, violent outbursts we see or read of in the daily paper, a drive to protect and heal seems integral to the constitution of human beings. Even though the sick are sometimes shunned and ill-treated, compassionate care for others is nonetheless a recurring theme of human history. While some may be disinclined to help suffering people, others regard care of the oppressed as an irrevocable part of their humanity: "One has to be an animal without a conscience not to help."[4] Because many people long for comfort and support themselves, they instinctively reach out to help others who are in need.[5] Woven into the intricate dark colors and disharmonies of life's tapestry is a sturdy luminous thread that binds all people together, lending integrity and endurance to the whole.

Some people who believe in God view this human tendency to give care as one of the qualities built into human nature by its Creator. It is a kind of divinely inspired compassion implanted by God to help people endure and thrive. Along with the typically recognized orders of government, family, and church,[6] there seems to be an order of social care whose main characteristic is to provide helping services to people in need. For want of a better term, we can call this order the "pastoral" order, and assign it a place alongside the standard orders of traditional theological thought.

The notion of a pastoral order throughout creation builds upon and enlarges the technical meaning of the pastoral office in the early church. In the emerging Christian community, positions of leadership naturally developed. These positions constituted a kind of pastoral office, and covered a wide variety of activities and services. The many gifts of leadership were described by an all-inclusive term, *diakonia*, or ministry. Leaders were "servants" or "ministers" (2 Cor. 3:6; Col. 1:25) who performed services of all sorts, including apostolic leadership, prophecy, teaching, working miracles, healing, helping, administering, and speaking in tongues (1 Cor. 12:27-28). A significant part of the *diakonia* or pastoral office in the early church was devoted to laying on hands to heal, and just helping those in need. The care of souls included visitation of the sick for their relief, both physical and spiritual. In the early and developing church, the office of healer was considered a "primary obligation of pastoral care."[7]

In its healing activities, the pastoral office exemplified in a new and especially illuminating manner the pastoral order God intends for all creation. The church brought into startlingly clear focus the kind of supportive mutuality that God willed and structured into all creation. The pastoral order focuses on the healing and helping functions of the pastoral office of the early church, and broadens the meaning of pastoral to include the supportive care of those in need provided by all people, not just the clergy. The pastoral order is that order ordained by God through which God calls all people to action in alleviating human suffering and blesses all with the mutual support of a caregiving community.

As with all the orders of creation, the pastoral order is embedded within the structures of reality. It is the order of helpful care that exists especially at the human level. Undergirding the common "order of Christian love"[8] there is a universal order of sympathetic interaction among all human beings. This order of active work alleviating suffering can be found in several of the major world religions and cultures, and particularly within Christianity.[9] It is this supportive relationship that is just the point in the various communities described in Scripture. According to the biblical story, woman is created to be a "helper" for man, and man is to cleave to woman with loving care (Gen. 2:20,24; Eph. 5:25; Col. 3:18-19). Children are to honor their parents (Exod. 20:12; Eph. 6:1), and parents are to provide for their children (Matt. 7:11). God calls a community of mutual service into being, which is to be a model for all people. In this community, God cares for the people (Exod. 14:29, 16:4), and the people are to respect and serve God and one another (Exod. 20:2-17; Is. 42:1-7; Mark 12:28-31; Acts 2:44-45). Human beings are made in the image of a Trinitarian God, a community of mutually supportive persons[10] that together create and care for the world and all its creatures. Caregiving is a part of the natural law written on the human heart by God.[11]

God creates the pastoral order insofar as God creates human beings for community. Wherever there is relationship there is the possibility of helpful care. Wherever God gives us a neighbor, a wife, a colleague, a student, a teacher, indeed, another human being, responsible interaction is implied. Furthermore, as with all the orders, the pastoral order is one way God blesses us through the things that are created. It is not a source of salvation, which is a gift of special revelation, but it is a means that God uses to enhance human life.

The blessings received, however, are limited by the temporal setting of the order. While God's will is revealed in the orders, God is also hidden within them. As part of the finite world, the pastoral order is marred by sin. Caregiving is often impeded by selfishness, insecurity, and anxiety. As there is strife in the family, corruption in government, and apostasy in the church, so there is laziness and insensitivity in the institutions and activities of the pastoral order. The Christian antidote to that blemish on the pastoral order is our next concern.

The Vocation of Caregiving

In his provocative book, *Waterbuffalo Theology*, Kosuke Koyama provides an Asian perspective on Christian themes. He suggests that Christians take seriously the Old Testament admonition to "love your neighbor as yourself" (Lev. 19:18). Indeed, "neighbourology" is more important than theology in the Asian context (1 John 4:20). It is necessary that we truly see our neighbor rather than treat him or her as an object. The reality of the neighbor, the need of the neighbor is the Christian's foremost concern. A neighborological approach will view the neighbor straightforwardly and avoid treating him or her as "maya" or illusion.[12]

Koyama describes life in the pastoral order as it is tempered by religious impulses. It is a life of genuine caring love of the other person. This takes place wherever people living in the pastoral order consciously understand and view their relationships in terms of vocation. It is possible that caregiving will occur in the pastoral order without a sense of vocation. Indeed, the nature of the pastoral order is to be the arena for helpful service between husband and wife, parents and children, and members of the same communities, as in the story of a young man who was the first on the scene of an automobile accident. He spotted a victim pinned under the wreckage, and with extraordinary strength he lifted the section trapping the victim, thereby allowing her to breathe. After the victim was safely taken to the hospital, the rescuer was interviewed. "I didn't think it was that big of a deal," he said. "I just did what anybody else would have done." The ready response to need is part of the equipment God supplies to everyone through the pastoral order. The caregiving supplied by that young man is indeed what anyone else would have tried to do with similar resolve and courage.

Caregiving takes place through all honorable "stations," such as those of husband, mother, clerk, judge, teacher — wherever a neighbor is given to us. In their particular "offices" of being a particular husband, mother, clerk, judge, or professor, people interact with others in supportive ways. Some stations and offices are especially supportive because they are explicitly dedicated to caregiving, such as the health professions, social services, and volunteer support. These stations and offices that cluster around suffering people do much good in the way of caregiving. They are particularly effective ways that God blesses us in the pastoral order.

However, there is an additional level or intensity to caregiving wherever it is recognized as a vocation.[13] A station or office becomes a vocation when it is understood as a calling from a gracious God to serve the neighbor in love. A sense of vocation adds to one's particular office as wife, son, attorney, or soldier a new sensitivity in caregiving that is given a particular shape and is accompanied by a special kind of support and hope. To understand one's office as vocation is to see it as both a calling from God by which we glorify God and a ministry of care by which we serve the neighbor.

All honorable offices bring glory to God through their embodiment of God's orders. An office discharged as a vocation, however, explicitly credits its origin and energy to God. At least the person having the vocation understands it as a calling from God, obedience to which is a service and honor to God. The caregiving implicit in the pastoral order, and in the health professions, for example, becomes a vocation when those who are its instruments see their caregiving as a calling from God and an expression of their religious convictions. An understanding of caregiving as a vocation is expressed by Kenneth Vaux when he says, "the whole enterprise of biomedicine is a theological response to the enigma of suffering."[14] For Vaux, at least, medical care is heavily freighted with religious weight, making it a form of vocation.

Also, an office becomes a vocation when it provides an *intentional* ministry of loving service to the neighbor.[15] Caregiving may convey love without expressing it. When caregiving is viewed as a vocation, the dimension of loving service is conscious and deliberate. The caregiver views his or her office as a means to the effective "neighbourology" that Koyama commends. It expresses the obedience called for by God in his command to love the neighbor as oneself, to care for the hungry, the poor, and the homeless as Jesus did in his ministry. Vocation makes real the intent in the pastoral order of providing works of love for those in need, and boldly explains the essential nature of the pastoral order as caring action on behalf of the suffering.

A Christian appropriation of the notion of vocation transforms that notion in a very special way. Our vocation not only becomes a calling from God to serve the neighbor in love; a Christian rendering of vocation adds the whole new dimension of cross-bearing to the concept.[16] The love that is an essential part of caregiving as a Christian vocation is a love willing to sacrifice security and comfort. It is a costly love, providing a service to the needy that is willing to go the second mile or give away the second cloak (Matt. 5:40-42). It is a love modeled after the love of Jesus, who sacrificed all on a cross dramatically to punctuate his life of selfless caregiving on behalf of others. The Christian is part of a community that is like a body in its mutual support of all its members (1 Cor. 12:25-26). The Christian contributes to the welfare of the whole without thought of personal reward (Mark 9:35).

And the Christian cares not only for the household of faith, but for all who are in need (Gal. 6:10). Freed by God's grace from all effort to save oneself, the caregiver can focus attention on saving (healing) others. This gives both breadth and depth to the caregiver's service as it reaches out in undistracted assistance to the distraught.[17] Caregiving as a Christian vocation serves the recipient of the care rather than the caregiver.[18] Christian caregivers fight for justice for others while bearing unjust persecution against themselves.[19] Caregiving as a Christian vocation attains its noblest expression as a service rendered to the needy without thought of benefit to the caregiver. It is the finest expression of life in the pastoral order, summed up by Gordon Jackson when he wrote, "The climax of pastoral caring is the ministry of the people of God who in response to a beckoning grace live beyond themselves in *radical love*."[20]

God's Support of Christian Caregiving

The notion of vocation is not particularly widespread in our current culture. Few people today understand their life or work in terms of vocation. A person making a survey of attitudes toward work today would likely find few people with a sense of calling in their work or a clear commitment to serving others in their occupation. Modern work largely justifies and serves the self, often exploits others, and seldom attains any transcendent meaning. Because of this secular domination of work, there is little sense of vocation in one's occupation or life. All semblances of a pastoral order are suffocated under the frenzied necessities of survival in a highly competitive market. Rare is the person who is able to rise above this dehumanizing structure and live a life of genuine caregiving.

The reasons for the eclipse of the pastoral order and the vocation of caregiving are many. However, let me suggest that one possible road to a recovery of the notion of caregiving as a vocation is through a restatement of God's care for us in our basic existence and in our efforts at caregiving. The pastoral order among people may become more viable the more we appreciate the support we enjoy from God, the ultimate Caregiver. Our vocation as caregivers to one another may be revitalized the more we realize how vitally God is the perfect Caregiver on our behalf.

In Part 2, we noted God's mighty acts of caregiving from creation through redemption to life eternal. Those actions alleviating suffering are the central exhibit in the believer's answers to the problem of evil. They are also a clue to the dynamics of human caregiving. All human caregiving depends upon God for its effectiveness. It is God who has both placed us in communities and put within us a sympathetic concern for one another. We come from the hand of God, made for a pastoral order that is also a gift of the Creator.

But there is a yet more radical way that God is within caregiving and supports those who do it. Whenever people consciously choose Christian caregiving as a vocation, they reflect the power and grace of God within them, enabling them to take up the cross of selfless service. While they may be set in a community with their natural sympathetic instincts toward others in that community intact, and while they may even fill the pastoral office of helpful mate or just manager, nevertheless, going the second mile in sacrificial service will not be a ready choice. To turn one's office or station into a vocation demands exceptional dedication and unselfishness. It requires the kind of obedience, love, and compassion of which saints are made.

Perhaps the image of the saint is just the way to explain the vocation of Christian caregiving: those who can attain it have been made capable of their service by the grace and strength of God. They are the "blessed" (Matt. 5:1-11) who are enabled to see things clearly and live according to that vision. They have been created anew as selfless caregivers by a power not of their own making. They have literally been brought into being from the things that were not.

The vocation of Christian caregiving is one among several cases in which God creates out of nothing. It is a particular instance of the fact that God sustains the world and all human accomplishment with creative grace. If that divine power were to cease, all things would disappear (Job 34:14-15). Further, the continuing dependence of the world upon God is an instance of creation out of nothing (Job 26:7-11; Ps. 104:24). Moreover, in doing the life-giving work of helping persons in need—the lowly, the wretched, the lost—God echoes the original, absolutely creative power. Most significant, the life of the redeemed is an action in which God creates out of nothing, first by negating all human efforts, and then by justifying persons who bring nothing in their favor to God.[21]

Wherever we see in action the vocation of Christian caregiving, especially there God is again creating something out of nothing. To be sure, there are some human ingredients operating in caregiving. It is part of the natural order to interact sympathetically with others. But it is not natural to relinquish one's comfort and well-being for the sake of the other. The kind of caregiving that bears a cross for others is the action of God within us. In such selfless caregiving, God is again doing God's marvelous work of creating out of nothing. Persons who are normally self-seeking and self-serving, who crumble under the weight of a cross of service, are empowered to live lives of servanthood. Persons who usually dream dreams of self-aggrandizement and shrink before the demands of service manage to turn outward in considerate care for others. Caregiving happens in spite of the relentless curvature of the self in upon itself. It happens by the might and mercy of a God who can bring out of nothing— human weakness and egocentricity—the something of service to others. As God is creator and provider in so many other ways, in this instance God creates and provides by placing in persons the freedom and resources necessary for the vocation of caregiving.

Perhaps the first step toward restoring the vocation of caregiving is to admit our need for help in fulfilling that vocation. While simple deeds of caregiving may be within our reach, the self-sacrifice involved in a vocation of caregiving takes the grace and greatness of God's Spirit within us. Where that Spirit is present, truly impressive caregiving can take place. Where that caregiving takes place, we see intimations of the God who can sustain us under the most demanding circumstances.

Sitting with a mother beside the bed of her comatose child, I discovered the courage God gives to caregivers. Critically wounded in an automobile accident, the child had not recovered consciousness or shown any signs of improvement for almost one month. Though brain-dead, the two-year-old had been kept alive through the tubes and wires that attached him to large life-supporting equipment. Realizing there was no conscious life in their child and that there was no hope for recovery, the parents decided to detach the life-support systems.

On the morning of the procedure, the mother reached into the small hospital bed, and for the first time in weeks held her child in her arms again. She sat in a rocking chair gently cradling her baby in her arms, offering what comfort might possibly be given. With a radiant composure she faced the worst that death can do, looked into eyes already vacant, grasped fingers that could no longer feel, held arms that were too weak to reach out. Surely she suffered unequaled pain and grief. Yet she stayed by her post, pouring out waves of love in one final goodbye.

The courage to face death, to minister as best one can in difficult circumstances and to do this out of loving compassion, reflects a strength and nobility of character beyond normal capacity. A mother's heart suffers grievously at such a moment. No loving care in life, no matter how thorough, can match that complete self-giving love in death. There can be no experience equal to it in depth of poignancy or height of bravery.

The image of that mother suffering with her dying son is the benediction of God over a world of pain and death. It is an echo of another death and another mother who cradled her son's broken body. The mother in that hospital was the *Pieta* of that intensive-care room. She carried in her soul the grief of a loss too great for human endurance. Yet she carried in her arms a love and compassion of divine dimension. Holding her son to her heart, comforting him through his last moments, she was a perfect instrument of caregiving. Her complete willingness to share an ordeal of shattering consequence revealed the power of love to conquer fear, an extraordinary strength that speaks of the very power of God (1 John 4:16-19).

CHAPTER NINE

The Biblical Call
to Caregiving

Religion can sometimes trap a person in a bog of abstract doctrines and theological beliefs, the endless discussion of which exhausts energy that could be given to active discipleship. One contemporary movement that tries to overcome that misapplied attention to things theoretical is liberation theology. Among other points, liberation theology emphasizes that Christianity is more than a belief system. Liberation theologians seek to shift the attention of Christianity away from mere understanding to significant transformation. Liberation theology focuses on *praxis* (or practice) rather than propositions, on actions rather than abstractions. The central images of liberation theology are the Exodus of Israel from slavery in Egypt and the liberating Christ, who calls his followers to a similar work of releasing the captives, especially those trapped in poverty by politically oppressive circumstances. Rather than a body of beliefs or a structure of doctrines, Christianity is a "form of discipleship in imitation of Christ."[1]

Christian caregiving expresses the spirit of liberation theology while broadening its focus beyond the political and economic realm. The care of suffering people is a major part of the call to Christian discipleship. To be a Christian is not merely to believe certain things, but also to practice a form of caring ministry in imitation of Christ. In addition to the general call given in the created order, then, there is a special call given to all who bear the name of Christ. In this chapter, we will examine more extensively the theme of caregiving as a Christian vocation. We will look at caregiving as practiced by those who believe in God, especially Christians. This will carry us into an exploration of the biblical and theological roots of caregiving and an overview of its general nature.

Action Preferred to Explanation

The biblical call to human action to alleviate suffering is set against a background of general disinterest in trying to explain or justify the existence of evil. There are only a few places in Scripture where any interest in a rationalistic approach to the problem surfaces. Job cries to God to explain why the good suffer and the wicked prosper (24:1), and particularly why he is a victim of God's anger (10:2). John records a brief dialogue between Jesus and the disciples over the reason for a blind man's affliction (John 9:1-3). Paul and James justify suffering on the basis of its utility (Rom. 5:3-5; James 1:2-4), and the author of 1 Peter links it to eternal life (5:10). Other than those few references, the Bible shows little interest in rational explanations of evil.

This is especially true in the ministry of Jesus. Once, when discussing a theological point with his disciples, Jesus directed attention away from the theoretical to the practical. The question was why temptations come to the faithful and whether or not God is the source of temptation. Jesus did not speculate on why temptations come, but warned against being the one who brings them (Luke 17:1-2; Matt. 18:6-7; see also 1 Cor. 10:13). Similarly, Jesus moved quickly from any discussion of why sickness comes to people to actions that alleviate sickness, as in his healing of the blind man, and in most of his healing miracles. Jesus seemed especially reluctant to rationalize suffering away.

It is generally recognized that Jesus was not so much a theoretician as a caregiver when confronting evil. "He never hinted that pain is *good in itself*: he healed the sick in body and mind, deeming pain a handicap or curse from which men should be delivered."[2] Jesus' style was to overcome suffering, not to use it.[3] Jesus was "dead set against" sickness, and wanted people to get over illness, not just to bear it.[4] Offering virtually no systematic discussion of why suffering exists, Jesus' approach was realistic and practical rather than theoretical and academic.[5] He confronted suffering and vanquished it.[6] Even in his preaching, ostensibly directed to his hearer's understanding, Jesus aimed at healing.[7] His proclamation was not so much an explanation of evil as an exorcism of evil. Finally, Jesus' resurrection was God's exclamation point on a life of practical victory over evil.[8]

The Biblical Call to Action

For the most part, Scripture is a call placed before the people of God to live a life of action in overcoming evil. This call is a logical consequence of God's prior action on behalf of the people. It is both a challenge and an opportunity for the disciples to provide a follow-up to that divine care by living a life of helpful service to others. Jesus stated this dynamic in general terms when he said to his followers, "As the Father has sent me, so I send you" (John 20:21).

Paul expresses the connection between God's caregiving action and human action clearly: As God has comforted us so we are to comfort others (2 Cor. 1:3-4). This equation was a central tenet of Jesus' teachings: "This is my commandment, that you love one another as I have loved you" (John 15:12). There was a sequential link between the healing actions of Jesus and the life of his followers. In a discourse meant to increase the faith and fortitude of the disciples, Jesus commended himself to his disciples on the basis of what he taught and what he did. Then, according to John, he added immediately, "Very truly, I tell you, the one who believes in me will also do the works that I do and, in fact, will do greater works than these, because I am going to the Father" (John 14:12). It seems apparent from these verses that human action to alleviate suffering is both commanded and empowered by God's action of the same order.

With God standing behind as guide and support, the envoy of God is to venture forth on a ministry of helping and healing. One form this ministry takes is that of struggling against all that oppresses people. With little penchant for theoretical discussion, the prophets call the people to action: "Cease to do evil, learn to do good" (Isa. 1:16-17); "Hate evil and love good, and establish justice in the gate. . . . Let justice roll down like waters, and righteousness like an everflowing stream" (Amos 5:15,24).

Similarly, Jesus called for action helping those who suffer. To the rich man he said, "Go, sell your possessions, and give the money to the poor" (Matt. 19:21). He called his disciples to a ministry of servanthood (Matt. 20:26). He commanded his followers to love their neighbors (Mark 12:31; Matt. 19:19, 22:39; Luke 10:27), and even their enemies (Matt. 5:44). He berated the scribes and Pharisees for neglecting "the weightier matters of the law: justice and mercy and faith" (Matt. 23:23). He offered his presence to the hungry and ill-clothed, the sick and imprisoned, and assured his followers that they could serve him by serving them (Matt. 25:34-40).

No story Jesus told makes the call to caregiving more clear than the parable of the Good Samaritan (Luke 10:25-37). With biting satire, Jesus lays out the scene. He shows a beaten and suffering traveler ignored by the upright and religious people who pass by him without lifting a finger to help. Then a foreigner, when he sees him, goes to him, dresses his wounds, carries him to a shelter, and puts him up for however long his recuperation will take. Who is the neighbor in this story? Jesus asks. When the lawyer correctly identifies the Samaritan because he was the one "who showed him mercy," Jesus tells him, "Go and do likewise." If there were any doubt in his followers' minds about their role as caregivers, this story would have erased it. It is a lucid and dramatic call to obey through our actions the command to love all who are in any need.

Jesus called his disciples to an active ministry of healing: "He appointed twelve . . . to be with him, and to be sent out to proclaim the message, and to have authority to cast out demons" (Mark 3:14-15). "Jesus summoned his twelve disciples and gave them authority over unclean spirits, to cast them out, and to cure every disease and every sickness" (Matt. 10:1; see also Mark 6:7 and Luke 9:1). "These twelve Jesus sent out with the following instructions: . . . Cure the sick, raise the dead, cleanse the lepers, cast out demons" (Matt. 10:5,8). To a wider group of seventy of the faithful he said, "Whenever you enter a town . . . cure the sick who are there" (Luke 10:8-9).

Several of Jesus' miracles involved a cooperative effort between

Jesus and the people. The healing occurs because of a joint application of empathy and energy. Perhaps the most elaborate of these miracles was the healing of the centurion's servant (Matt. 8:5-13). First, there was the concern of the officer for his dear servant. This is implemented by a group of elders who approached Jesus for help. As Jesus follows the elders to the servant, he is met by another contingent with a message not to bother coming any farther, but merely to give the command for the servant's recovery. Jesus obliged because of the centurion's faith, and when they returned home the servant was well again.

We can't know for certain, but there may have been a dozen people involved in that miracle. Other people who were cured through a joint effort between Jesus and human caregivers include the paralytic let down through a roof (Mark 2:1-12), Jairus's daughter (Mark 5:21-24,35-43), the royal official's son (John 4:46-54), and those brought to Jesus by the people of Gennesaret and others near the Sea of Galilee (Mark 6:53-56; Luke 4:40). The ready help of great numbers of people is a vital part of many cures at the hands of Jesus.

In the lives of the disciples and the leaders of the early church, healings occur as a routine part of the ministry. Jesus passed on the power to heal to his disciples (Matt. 10:1; Mark 6:7). This power enabled a widespread healing ministry that touched the lives of many people (Mark 6:13; Luke 9:6). Although their healing power did not always work (Mark 9:18), healings were an important part of the apostolic witness. Jesus promised the apostles that the gift of healing would be among the signs that he would grant them after his death (Mark 16:17-18), and indeed the Acts of the Apostles records a number of such healing miracles occurring at the hands of Peter and John (3:1-10), Paul (14:8-10, 19:11-12, 28:7-9), and Philip (8:4-8). Acts also records that Peter and Paul each raised a person from the dead (9:36-41, 20:9-12).

The Reciprocity of Faith

It is generally recognized today that as a "matching grant" consequence of God's care, a ministry of alleviating suffering is an essential part of Christian discipleship. As God has cared for us and helped us, so we are to care for and help others in God's name.

"Compassion is a hallmark of our discipleship and the sign of God's care for us. . . . It expresses our decision to stand by another, as God in his agape love steadfastly determines to stand by us."[9] Having been healed, we can heal others.[10] It is God who makes caregivers, God's caregiving serving as the impetus and model for creature caregiving. As Kenneth Haugk expresses it, "I believe that Jesus cares for me so much that he was willing to give his life for me. Remembering his love, I can't help but reach out and share that love and care with others."[11]

The explicit example of the reciprocity of faith is the life of Jesus, who "adopted a servant style in his own ministry and told his disciples to follow his example."[12] Jesus was among his followers "as one who serves" (Luke 22:27). His mission was "to serve, and to give his life as a ransom for many" (Matt. 20:28). In the setting of the Last Supper, Jesus declared that the leader will be one who serves (Luke 22:26), and provided dramatic punctuation for this teaching by washing the disciples' feet (John 13:4-11).

There was to be a direct correlation between the works of Jesus and the works of his followers: "He spoke often of his ministry as one of service and laid down the same pattern for the ministry of his disciples."[13] He taught them that the servant is not above the master or the disciple above the teacher (Matt. 10:24-25; Luke 6:40), that whoever would be great must be servant and whoever would be first must be last (Mark 9:35, 10:42-45; Matt. 23:11). The disciples were to follow Jesus' example, "just as the Son of Man came not to be served but to serve" (Matt. 20:28). The early Christians understood this servant role of Jesus and the necessity for servanthood in their ministry. For them Jesus was the Lord who "emptied himself, taking the form of a slave" (Phil. 2:7). Likewise those who were leaders in the church were to devote themselves to "the service of the saints" (1 Cor. 16:15). This was to be, however, an active servanthood of overcoming evil with good (Rom. 12:21), and gaining victory over the world for those who believe (1 John 4:4).

Jesus' acts of caregiving become the model for the actions of those who follow his ways. Jesus' life of love, hope, and faith are carried on by those who administer loving care to others. Jesus embodied a multifaceted practice of healing in his hands, feet, and eyes. We see in his eyes a person perceiving the way for total salvation of those around him. We see in his feet the steps of one who opposes the codes of his day and teaches equality and servanthood. We see in his hands a constant reaching out to heal the sick and feed the hungry. Jesus' practice of faith, hope, and love is laid upon the church as its own practice. Christology is to become ecclesiology as Jesus' own example of action becomes the church's example to follow.[14] Thus, caregiving is an essential part of the comprehensive effort to bear Christ's action in the world today.

All these insights about ministry add up to a dynamic we might call "reciprocity." The call to action in alleviating suffering is part of the reciprocity of Christian faith. Human action overcoming evil is the reply in kind to God's action overcoming evil on our behalf. The servant role of caregiver is the mirror image of the divine Servant who gave all in care of us. The one who would be great, Jesus said, must be servant of all, a posture he himself assumed with the disciples. As Jesus was servant to those around him and Savior to all, so those who follow his way are to be caregivers to others around them.

The call to take up arms in the struggle against evil is the matching response to the gospel story of God's battle against the great tyrants. The showdown of that contest was on the cross, where Jesus finally defeated sin, death, and the devil. That sacrifice and ultimate victory was for us and for our salvation. It was the supreme instance of divine caregiving on our behalf. God the unsurpassable caregiver won the battle over evil and suffering so that we might attain a similar victory. The cross was the instrument through which Jesus suffered in our stead in order that we could have a chance to defeat the tyrants in our life, and thereby reduce the level of suffering we would otherwise have to endure.

Human care of others is the reciprocal response to God's care of us. As Jesus stood in our stead on the cross, just so we are to stand in his stead in the world today, bringing healing and wholeness to those around us. As he shared in the sufferings of the world on the cross for us, so we share in the sufferings of the world today for him. Human caregiving is a return in kind for the care God has shown toward us. It is the way we can re-present Christ's healing ministry in the present world. Those who supply Christian caregiving are the body of Christ in the world: his substitute, proxy, representative. They stand in his stead bearing the cruciform shape of his life in the world today.

The action of caregiving is an essential part of the rhythm of the

Christian drama. That drama is one story in two acts. First, we see Christ suffering in our stead on the cross that we might be saved; second, we see the disciples suffering in the world that Christ might be remembered. Christ the Good Shepherd calls the disciples to be shepherds for others. Christ the Prince of Peace makes his disciples peacemakers in the world. Christ the Great Physician, who healed broken bodies and lives, continues to heal through the disciples living in a wounded world today. Caregiving is the human complement of a divine activism expended on the world to save it, to heal it and restore it to wholeness.

Co-Helping in Caregiving

While caregiving is a universal order commanded by God in creation and evident to some degree in all cultures, the special call that comes through the Bible and Christianity in particular has prompted special effort at compassionate caregiving among Christians. This active reciprocity is evident in the growth of orders and institutions of caregiving where Christian influence has been effective. The practice of nursing, the development of hospitals, and the emergence of medicine have received significant impetus from Christian sources,[15] attesting to the central place that caregiving occupies in the Christian scheme.

The Christian effort at caregiving also adds weight to the proposal for an activist solution to the problem of evil. The Christian gospel offers a clear and feasible program for writing a credible theodicy. It is an invitation to realize the true meaning of "holiness," namely a "co-creative role with God in alleviating human suffering and making justice in the world."[16]

The Christian drama is staged to include the efforts of human beings in unravelling its meaning. The answer to suffering is not a *Deus ex Machina*, a mechanical deity suddenly lowered into the human scene to solve all its problems. The answer is found in the willing cooperation of human beings who serve as the hands, feet, and eyes of Jesus in the world today. The biblical call to caregiving offers the privilege of "participating in the work of a compassionate God whose agenda is the mending of all creation."[17] In that co-creative work, that sharing of the burden of healing all creation, lies the most hopeful solution to the intellectual problem of evil.

CHAPTER TEN

Discipleship As Caregiving

In the previous chapter we considered the nature of the biblical call to caregiving. In this chapter we will focus on the scope of the mandate to serve others. We will look at caregiving as the whole of the discipleship of the whole congregation to the whole of human life. Four areas of discipleship will come under our review: ecological care, social care, intellectual care, and personal care.

First, let us recall our theme and the direction we have been moving. I have suggested that the solution to the intellectual problem of evil is to be found in actions to alleviate suffering. The theological base and impetus for this action is the story of God's care for us as this story comes to us from Scripture. Building on that foundation, an activist approach to the problem of evil will seek to reduce human suffering in the world today. The solution, therefore, exists in the form of a call issued through the created order and Christian discipleship in particular.

The answer to the problem of suffering exists largely as a challenge to take up those actions that will overcome suffering. What follows, therefore, is a description of the optimum nature of caregiving and several desirable examples for society today. It is the style of discipleship toward which we must move if there is to be any relief for the spiritual anguish present in suffering. Discipleship in helpful service is the crux of the issue. We must recognize the inclusive scope and the extensive reach of caregiving. Just as healing was never merely incidental to Jesus' message,[1] so it is integral to the ministry of the church today. Indeed, caregiving is what discipleship is all about.[2] Rather than expressing one aspect of discipleship, caregiving is another definition of discipleship. It is the *whole of ministry*. All aspects of ministry—preaching, worship, teaching, counseling, and service—are forms of caregiving. Preaching is giving care to those who seek the peace of God. Worship is filling the deep springs of the spirit with the "water of life." Teaching is caring for the understanding and commitment of the believer. Counseling is healing the wounds of those who have been broken by the world. Service is offering opportunities for those who hunger and thirst for righteousness. Healing is not so much one part of the ministry as it is a description of ministry in its broadest impact. Where there is no caregiving, it is fair to say, there is no ministry.

Not only is caregiving the whole of the church's ministry, it is the *ministry of the whole church*. The work of caregiving, spiritual or otherwise, is not the work of the clergy alone. While the pastoral office may specify particular forms of caregiving, pastoral care is the work of the whole congregation. It is "that care for another given by any active and faith-filled member of the Christian community."[3] Established concepts about ministry take on new shape in the light of a caregiving mentality. Pastoral theology is not the exclusive domain of the clergy leader, but, to the contrary, is informed by the caregiving work of the whole congregation, of which professional ministerial care is a subordinate part.[4] Based on Jesus' extension of the healing ministry to his disciples, the church ought to be a community of care where "everyone must then realize that he is called...to the healing ministry in the name of Jesus, the Saviour of men."[5]

In the third place, not only is caregiving the whole of discipleship discharged by the whole of the believing community: it is also directed to the *whole of the human condition*. Caregiving is not confined merely to spiritual needs or the religious fellowship. While Paul says we should care "especially for those of the family of faith," he also says we should "work for the good of all" (Gal. 6:10). Caregiving reaches into the world where it confronts "all sorts and conditions" of people: "Biblically and practically, pastoral care is the mutual concern of Christians for each other and for those in the world for whom Christ died."[6] When expressed in the world, caregiving will confront a great variety of suffering people: "If the Church would be true to its Lord today, it must be rooted theologically in the Kingdom and express its theology in a deep commitment to, and outgoing concern for, the sick, the refugees, the underprivileged, the prisoners, the outcast, the poor."[7] This means that caregiving will take on a variety of forms according to the needs that it addresses.[8] Following are four examples of the different shapes that caregiving can take when it reaches out to the many faces of human suffering.

Ecological Caregiving

One way Christian discipleship can address the intellectual problem of evil is through concern for the care of the whole of creation. The abuse of the natural world causes untold suffering among both humans and animals. For increasing numbers of people, nature is perceived as having intrinsic value and the violation of nature is felt to be a fundamental wrong against something that has the right to survive and thrive. Many human beings openly grieve over the ecological crimes committed against the environment. In the human order, abuse and neglect of the environment brings unemployment, a shortage of crops and goods, loss of aesthetic and recreational resources, forced displacement, and a feeling of profound despair. More serious, the very life of the human community is threatened by pollution, the elimination of food supplies, and shrinking energy resources. Trauma to the environment is trauma to those who live within it. Action to protect and preserve the natural world is action to ease the burden of human suffering in that world. It is one way to do something to solve the intellectual problem of evil.

One Christian who has taken his discipleship into the ecological realm is Wesley Granberg-Michaelson. President of the New Creation Institute and a practicing evangelical, Granberg-Michaelson is concerned that the church has not been fully alert to the ecological crisis or its own responsibility in dealing with that crisis. The crisis has caused enormous suffering throughout the world to both the natural and human order. The loss of forests, destruction of plants, and decimation of animal life have ripped a huge gash across the earth. Increases in toxic chemical pollution have poisoned thousands of people and led to countless deaths. The abundance of packaging materials and other household garbage has produced a trash problem of gargantuan proportions.[9] All these forms of environmental deterioration degrade and destroy human life and add heavy burdens to the load of human suffering.

Granberg-Michaelson suggests a multiple approach to the problem. First, since the mess we are in has been caused in part by the failure of the church to do its theological homework, the initial step must be a recovery of biblical and theological roots. In particular, we need a return to biblical wisdom that teaches that creation is good, God is the Creator, and the earth is included in God's redemptive plan. It is not the case, as some have argued, that Western culture has been captive to nature-denying Christian influences. Rather, it is that the church has been captive to the non-theological, abusive technology of the modern world. It is time, therefore, to recover the biblical view of nature as God's creation with intrinsic worth and vital significance in the scheme of redemption.

This attention to the theological base, however, is only the preparation for Christian action directed at overcoming the problem. Granberg-Michaelson describes his personal activist answer: a compost pile for recycling grass clippings, kitchen waste, and spoiled produce. He also provides a list of Christian groups, conferences, and projects involved in earthkeeping: Recycle Unlimited, AuSable Trails Institute of Environmental Studies, Sierra Treks, Ecumenical Task Force of the Niagra Frontier, Eco-Justice Working Group, North American Conference on Christianity and Ecology, Christian Farmers Federation in Canada, missionary earthkeeping, and the World Council of Churches.[10] The implication in listing these groups is clear: the Christian is called to preserve and renew nature through *participation* in the works of preservation and renewal. The answer to this mess we are in is involvement in some project to straighten out the mess and get the human race back on an environmentally responsible track.

In an appendix, Granberg-Michaelson includes several important writings on the ecological crisis. Vincent Rossi argues that the way ahead is through a recovery of the notion of servanthood. This notion, which as we have already noted, plays such an important part in an activist theodicy translates out to the concept of stewardship in the environmental realm. Stewardship, for Rossi, "may be the only effective platform for a deep ecology movement."[11] Stewardship, of course, is the active and responsible care of the earth by responsible managers of its resources. Out of this action of doing something to help the environment may come that "substantial healing" of which Francis Schaeffer writes: "When the church puts belief into practice, in man *and in nature*, there is substantial healing."[12] Beliefs put into action provide the way to healing for Schaeffer. And it is healing that is the goal. Thus, the emergency care of nature, and human beings within nature, is one area where a discipleship of caregiving addresses the intellectual problem of evil.

Social Caregiving

A second realm where active effort to alleviate human suffering is a ray of light in the midst of the darkness of evil is the political and social order. There is little question that the very arena that should be the place of mutual service, namely the social order, is more often than not shattered by conflict and destruction. This suffering is especially widespread and acute in the workplace.

One Christian observer who has poignantly documented the pain that affects and plagues the worker is Dorothee Soelle. According to Soelle, the burden of suffering associated with employment and production is both physical and psychological. Working conditions often assault the body and its senses, causing painful wear and tear. And work afflicts people with severe psychological woes: a feeling of degradation because of isolation and impersonality, deadening boredom due to the repetition of monotonous tasks, a loss of control, an overwhelming sense of helplessness in the face of dehumanizing circumstances, and a nagging hopelessness from a situation that seems absolutely resistant to change.[13] Work not only attacks the individual but destroys human relationships. It is a treadmill going nowhere that alienates the worker from his or her neighbor. Instead of a paradise, it is often a curse or punishment that humiliates human dignity beneath lesser values and ambitions. In particular, where profit and production are the only ambition, greed, envy, and avarice prostitute the human community, destroying solidarity and relatedness.[14]

Soelle is insistent that the way to deal with this social suffering is not to try to explain it or live with it. Soelle has no use for such rational theodicies. She rejects any hint that God sends suffering or any reasoning that makes suffering a test or expiation, saying that all such interpretations are wicked and a mockery of genuine horrible suffering.[15] There is a very good reason Soelle is so adamant against efforts to explain evil away. If we make suffering too acceptable, we will never work for change that overcomes it. If we learn too much from it, we will miss the message that evil is bad and must be eliminated.[16] To do so would be to forfeit our biblical heritage and Christian duty. Scripture is clear that the strategy with suffering is not to explain it but to get free from it. The task of the Christian in the face of evil is not to talk about it, but to abolish the circumstances that cause it. If we don't take an active role against evil, then we become part of the evil ourselves.[17]

If the goal is to alleviate suffering, then what are the components in that strategy? Interestingly, Soelle lists speech as one of the first steps in overcoming evil. However, this speech is not composed of arguments justifying evil, but complaints and laments against the pain that it brings. To suffer mutely without the chance even to verbalize one's pain is the worst of all situations. To talk about one's pain, to cry out in protest, is to open the door to escape. In this task, religion can give form to speech through prayer and liturgy.[18] However, the next step is absolutely essential. One must walk through the door and away from suffering. One must "organize to conquer suffering," to take action against it. Active behavior must replace purely reactive behavior. In the struggle against evil, we are to be God's hands to act on behalf of others in the fight against suffering.[19]

The only way to deal with suffering is to struggle against it. In the workplace this can take the shape of reform and reconstruction of the work situation. We must redesign work so that it gives expression to our humanity rather than destroying it. We must structure work so that it assists the needy rather than exploits them.[20] All these efforts are expressions of Christian discipleship as caregiving. The believer is one who does not submit to suffering, but takes up arms against it. To be sure, this struggle against evil may entail suffering for the caregiver as a by-product of his or her action. But this useful suffering is a triumphant suffering that is not to be confused with submissive or senseless suffering.[21]

Intellectual Caregiving

There is a saying that life is a tragedy for those who think and a comedy for those who feel. Surely few people experience the tragic dimension of life more keenly than those who think about God. Such thinking confounds the believer with paradox and unproven claims. It requires believing some things for which there is little or no evidence and making sense of other things that are self-contradictory. Anyone who chooses to be a reflective believer is doomed to a life of constant intellectual frustration and disappointment. It is a life lived in the midst of unresolved contradictions and undocumented assertions. It is a life in which the believer forfeits all rational certainty for the sake of the treasures of faith. For many thinking Christians this crucifixion of reason entails profound and lasting suffering.

There is another kind of suffering associated with theology. This is suffering caused by the seeming irrelevance of the whole effort of making sense of religion. Not only is the course of theology likely to lead to failure, the entire enterprise seems futile in the first place. For many people, theology is an irrelevant and useless enterprise, an exercise in semantics and rhetoric. Particularly in this current age there seems to be little interest in the cognitive beliefs of religion. It is the experiential and sensational aspects of religion that catch the attention of people today.[22]

Part of the reason for this turn to folk religion (as distinguished from formal religion) is a disillusionment with the work of theology. This disillusionment is bred from many sources — empiricism, relativism, scientism, nihilism — but includes the perception that the academic study of religion is woefully abstract and inconsequential. The popular view is that theology is a discipline for ivy halls and remote towers with little relevance to the real world. Theologians seem to talk only to other theologians in journals that only those in the profession can understand. This widespread judgment that writes theology off as of no consequence causes pronounced suffering among theologians who take their work seriously. Their pain is sometimes evident in the complaints of theologians that church people aren't interested in theology. This divide between theologians and the church also deprives the church of resources that could be of important help to it and further compounds the suffering that the faithful endure in their life in the world.

The suffering of the church in its intellectual life is an arena for Christian caregiving. It is a part of Christian discipleship to comfort those who anguish over the impossibility and the irrelevance of Christian beliefs. This caregiving can take various forms, but a form consonant with activist proclivities would provide a way to overcome the sources of the problem. This would not be so much another abstraction as an action. Effective Christian caregiving for those who do theology and for the church that suffers the absence of a meaningful theology should take the form of changing that theology so it becomes more vital in the life of the church. It is not in more discussion of the formal subjects of theology that an answer lies, but in a transformation of theology toward a practical program of witness and service. Compassionate caregiving of the theological community, both in its work and in its impact on the church, should revitalize the enterprise of theology so that it is a respected and significant part of the believing fellowship.

Just such a re-formation of theology is the plan of Douglas John Hall. He suggests that there is a "disturbing connection between the failure of professional theology to think comprehensively and contextually, and the spirit of anti-intellectualism present within the churches."[23] If the church is suffering under an attack of anti-intellectualism (anti-theology), it is because the church has brought the attack upon itself. Generations of abstract, academic theology that have neglected the real mission of the church has led to a wholesale dismissal of theology as beside the point, namely, the point of what the church ought to be about. Hall is not about to give up the thinking side of faith, however. He is clear that thinking is an essential part of religious belief. Christianity is a faith that must be thought, and only a thinking faith can survive in the world today.[24] Hall is not one to abandon theology and join the anti-intellectuals.

However, the way ahead, Hall suggests, is not to somehow think *harder*. The malady is not that the church has been sloppy in its homework. The solution is not more of the same academic exercises. Rather, the solution to the suffering of theology in its schools and churches is to revolutionize its shape. We must take action to change the focus of theology. Moreover, the focus of theology must shift from the abstract to actual. Thus, there is a twofold turn to action. In the action of changing theology, theology must change itself into an *action-oriented* discipline. It must become a "praxis theology" that practices what it teaches and seeks its place in the world among those who are suffering. It must do its work in the midst of the actual terrors and trials that beset people. Theology must rethink its mandate in view of the darkness that engulfs the world, the awful struggles of oppressed and broken people. Theology must face its own crucifixion in a world of daunting challenges to faith. Its mission is to state anew the centrality of the cross in the life of the faithful.[25]

The care that the intellectual life of the church needs, therefore, is care that it may not welcome. To change its focus from seeking security to identifying with the emptiness is a *metanoia* (turning around) of major proportions. But it is this radical revision that is the ultimate solution to its internal malaise and the bad press that it is receiving. If theology wants to overcome the suffering within its ranks and in the church due to its detachment from and disregard by the world, it will have to be willing to take on another kind of suffering, that of a comprehensiveness and immediacy that locates it within the ambiguity and pain of the world. This change, however, is the recovery and salvation of theology as it rediscovers its true nature. There is a centering and a healing that is truly a victory over the dissolution and decay of its previous life. Useless suffering has been overcome and replaced by a useful suffering. Christian caregiving has accomplished its goal through a triumph of the spirit that reintegrates and resurrects theology to a new life.

Personal Caregiving

Because we are physical beings, the greatest bulk of human suffering arises from bodily disease, illness, injury, disability, and infirmity, and the psychological and emotional stress that they cause. Everyone has some contact, if only secondhand, with human suffering. Few people will live a life free from at least one bout with personal suffering. Whether caused by genetics, accident, life-style, old age, or impending death, personal suffering spares almost no one. Moreover, it is often a frequent visitor in the homes of many people who experience multiple tragedies and ailments in their lives. It is so recurring in some cases that it becomes the dominant motif in life, perhaps calling forth a style of coping and a level of courage that are an inspiration to many. This fundamental level of suffering comprises a huge arena for Christian caregiving.

One evidence of the universal scope of personal suffering is the abundance of literature about it. Bookstores and libraries are packed with books telling a woeful tale of pain, disease, and death, and the human drama surmounting such suffering. Denominational magazines regularly publish stories of great faith and fortitude in the face of terrible suffering. Talk shows feature authors of best-sellers about Herculean triumph over personal tragedy. One writer who is very familiar with this dramatic landscape is Erika Schuchardt. She has studied five hundred cases of all sorts and conditions of suffering, most in the last two decades. Her account provides an excellent baseline for talking about personal suffering, and confirms the action-oriented approach advocated in this book.

With five hundred case studies as background, and six stories reviewed in more detail, Schuchardt argues for the importance of social integration in coping with suffering. In order to reach that goal, however, the afflicted person must go through several stages of crisis management. These are divided into three learning phases having to do with cognitive adjustment, emotional growth, and action taken to manage suffering. Schuchardt found that where sufferers go through all phases, including the expression of aggression, they are likely to reach the target of successful coping. In the liberation of aggression, Christian faith can be a vital catalyst. Support givers can play an important role in helping sufferers utilize their faith for that purpose. They can also provide help to the sufferer so that together they take control of the crisis.

It is in the action of working through the insecurity, anger, and despair, among other things, of the sufferer that a Christian approach to suffering lies. Schuchardt discovered that rationalizations of suffering were of no help to sufferers. Talk of sickness as a religious privilege or a punishment, or the offer of heaven as a reward, were answers that did not answer.[26] Schuchardt chides the church for too often taking an insipid theological approach to suffering rather than a compassionate pastoral approach. There are no answers to the "whys and wherefores" of suffering. Caregivers who proceed by "quoting comforting Bible verses and theological arguments" really block the process of crisis management.[27] Citing A. M. K. Müller, Schuchardt notes that theories negate temporality whereas sickness reveals our bondage to time.[28] This suggests that sufferers are little impressed by abstract theology and are more interested in what is actually happening to them and in forming some supportive relationships.

Because Schuchardt is dealing with cases with little hope for a cure, she strongly emphasizes reaching a stage of acceptance. In this process Christian faith is helpful as a format facilitating the expression of anger. It would seem that this is all mere theoretical or theological adjustment. In fact, Schuchardt makes this process a joint action between the sufferer and the caregiver. It is the caregiver's role to help the sufferer move through the action of crisis management to the goal of solidarity. While this involves some cognitive content, the caregiver is present not as a theoretician but as a companion who actively assists the sufferer in a catharsis of faith.[29] Genuinely helpful caregiving facilitates the action of release from crippling thoughts and negative feelings so that the sufferer can move on to the final stage of solidarity.

Schuchardt also does not consider acceptance as in any way sanctioning suffering. She cites Luther as an authority who counsels a struggle against destructive forces.[30] The whole point of the movement to solidarity is to reach a stage of management *within the parameters of reality*. As noted, Schuchardt is dealing with severe, seemingly incurable sickness and disability, and the action she proposes is circumscribed by those intractable facts. Nevertheless, she does not think sufferers or caregivers should settle down with the suffering as a burdensome limitation. The point of moving through the phases is to reach a stage of "activity" where the sufferer decides to make the best of it. This then leads to the final stage of solidarity in which sufferer and caregiver work together to take control of the crisis.[31] Presumably this includes taking action to live as full and active a life as possible, in effect denying suffering any rights. It is the ministry of the Christian caregiver to stand with the sufferer in turning back the debilitating and discouraging effects of the illness or disability. This is not a passive acceptance, but an active acceptance that will not let suffering have the last word.

Conclusion

Christian caregiving in the midst of ecological, social, intellectual, and personal suffering is a style of theodicy that the church would do well to adopt. It is a strategy that is central to the meaning of discipleship. In carrying out a caregiving ministry, the church is doing only what it is called to do. The "mutual conversation and consolation" of the brethren is woven into the very fabric of life together in the faith. The call to love the neighbor as oneself is the guiding standard of life in the world.

Caregiving at all levels of interaction in the church gathered and the church scattered is the distinct mark of Christian discipleship. Therefore, the church need look no further than its own nature as a caring community for an answer to the intellectual problem of evil. It has within its own structure and mission the appropriate response to the problem. All it needs to do is activate its servant role in the various regions where caregiving is needed in order to handle that problem.

The challenge of the different levels of caregiving outlined in this chapter is also the opportunity for the church to make a meaningful statement about the Christian approach to evil. The solution to that problem is not lost in the endless detours of academic debate, but hidden in the very vision and action of Christian discipleship. Let us look, finally, at how discipleship in caregiving, particularly in the personal arena, is a "statement" resolving the intellectual problem of evil.

PART FOUR

Carevision and the
Problem of Evil

CHAPTER ELEVEN

God As Companion, Not Cause

What difference does carevision make? Carevision builds an ecology of care out of biblical foundations (Part 2), and deeds of mercy (Part 3). Carevision is envisioning the deeds as the superstructure for the theological foundation. But just what does providing care say about suffering, God, and the ultimate order of things? In this final section, we will look at possible implications of caregiving for the problem of evil. What kind of statement does carevision make both to the care receiver and the care provider? I want to suggest that it speaks far more effectively than our usual words on this subject.

A little-known hymn of the church begins:

> O Christ, the healer, we have come
> To pray for health, to plead for friends.
> How can we fail to be restored
> When reached by love that never ends?[1]

---

[1] O CHRIST, THE HEALER. Words: Fred Pratt Green. Words copyright © 1969 by Hope Publishing Co., Carol Stream, IL 60188. All rights reserved. Used by permission.

To be restored, to attain to health and wholeness is the prayer of the faithful for themselves and others. Moreover, it is a hopeful plea, buoyed up by the testimony to God's love found in Scripture and history. This love is endless in capacity and in expanse. God has resources sufficient to heal the world of all its pain. These resources are as available today as in biblical times. However, it is only through the ministry of believing caregivers that God's love becomes practically effective in this time. Moreover, it is this action of compassionate caregiving that speaks credibly to the intellectual problem of evil. The statement that such caregiving makes to that problem is the subject of this and the remaining chapters.

A New Way of Thinking

The suggestion that caregiving actions can speak to the intellectual problem of evil faces stubborn misconceptions about the nature and importance of pastoral care. For one thing, caregivers themselves sometimes shortchange the importance of their caregiving in the total picture. A chaplain writes, "The way that I'm different from everybody else in this hospital is that my main job is to *be* with the patients. . . . Everybody else who comes in the sick room has to *do* something to or for the patient. All I have to do is to be there."[2] Granting the intrinsic value of *being* with the patient (and we will have more to say about this shortly), to fail to see this ministry of presence as *doing* something to and for the patient is to devalue the impact of such caregiving. The act of being with a suffering person, and a whole host of nonprofessional acts of caregiving, can be as important to the patient as the actions of people who officially do something to and for the patient.

The second habit of thinking that must be overcome if we are to appreciate the statement caregiving makes is the perception that medicine focuses exclusively on the removal of suffering and religion concentrates solely on understanding its meaning. Joseph Fichter expresses this way of thinking when he writes, "If religion strives to understand the meaning of pain and the reasons why suffering continues to be a widespread human experience, medical science strives to get rid of pain, or to alleviate it as far as possible."[3] To be sure, there are significant differences in approach and professional boundaries should be maintained, but to divide the tasks of science and religion so neatly is not always helpful. Medical knowledge about pain and its treatment can aid reflection about its meaning. As this whole book argues, the activist side of religion is, or ought to be, very much interested in reducing the pain of sufferers. Moreover, it is just as religion turns activist in its approach to suffering that it is able to wring any meaning out of that pain. In the same way, medicine is a kind of devotion in its very action of reducing pain.[4] It would seem that each approach is enriched when seen in the light of the other, instead of being rigidly separated from the other.

As faith active in love, Christian caregiving has much to say about the problem of evil, but in the inverse of what we have come to know in philosophy as "speech-acts." Some of the things that we say are statements of our intention to live a certain kind of life: ethical and religious language, especially, is linked to behavior. When we say, "I believe in God," we are confessing our intention to live our life as a believer. Our words are shorthand for our actions. In an activist approach to suffering and evil, our actions are shorthand for our words. It is by the acts we perform that we say something about reality and our place within in. Through acts of caregiving, we declare our solution to the intellectual problem of evil. The care-filled performance of deeds of love "sum up" all we want to say about suffering, our place within it, and God's relationship to it. If much of our language is "speech-acts," icons for actions, much of our caregiving is "acts-speech," icons for concepts or messages. By our loving efforts to overcome evil, we seek a theodicy that we believe is intelligible and cogent.

In our study of the statement that caregiving makes concerning the problem of evil we will look at caregiving in the *personal* arena among people who suffer sickness, injury, and disability. Although the scope of caregiving is broad, we will focus on the personal realm mainly because resources in this area are available and abundant. And we will concentrate on *Christian* caregiving. If caregiving is to speak to the intellectual problem of evil, it must somehow convey the fact that it is done "in the name of God." This is not to say that only religious people can effectively give care, but that if caregiving is to speak to the question of God's implication in suffering, the caregiving must somehow be perceived as an expression of God's will. Such a connection need not always be explicit, but only that the caregiver be recognized as a believer, whatever that may involve. Since the problem exists for faith, only an answer that arises within faith can be effective.

Often when people encounter the problem of suffering and evil, they voice their concerns in the form of *questions*. While the focus of these questions is usually God's implication in suffering, the way the questions surface will vary in particulars. Typically, they arise in the form of personal, existential questions. These questions open for us a way to consider several of the implications of caregiving for the problem of evil. We will look at one question in this chapter and two additional questions in the following two chapters.

"Why me, Lord?"

Among the questions that suffering gives rise to is the personal lament, "Why me?" This question arises in part because of the terrible isolation that often accompanies sickness. Typically, people who are sick are "isolated from their families, friends, work, and meaningful activities."[5] Sickness also creates feelings of loneliness within the patient, as in this woman's reflection following surgery: "When they came to wheel me into the operating room and I said goodbye to my husband and daughter, I couldn't stop thinking that this must be what dying is like. You're so alone. No one can do it for you. No one can go through it with you, not really."[6]

Similar testimony can be heard throughout hospitals and in all kinds of sickness. Pain and disability are intensely personal experiences that create the perception in the sufferer that no one else can understand what he or she is going through. This in turn makes the sufferer feel as though he or she is uniquely required to endure suffering. A young doctor diagnosed with cancer expressed it this way: "I was feeling lonely and isolated. . . . In my mind I was the only one who had been struck down with the kind of mortal illness that I associated with the elderly."[7]

The other ingredient in the question "Why me?" is a feeling that one has been singled out by God to undergo suffering. Persons who have been burdened with illness often feel victimized. As part of their aloneness, they feel distanced not only from colleagues, family, and friends, but also from God. They wonder, Why did God pick on me? What did I do to deserve to be punished in this way? Even people who are not particularly devout worry about the wider implications of their illness. The young doctor with cancer asked, "Was I a victim of the supernatural — some malevolent and vindictive force disseminated by chain letter? . . . What act of hubris had I been guilty of? . . . What had I done wrong?"[8]

The onslaught of illness and its terrible effect of isolating the sufferer physically, emotionally, and spiritually can create excruciating doubt about the good nature of God. The paranoia that lurks in the shadows of loneliness can erupt in severe recriminations against God. Instead of a caring presence, God becomes a cohort in the crime of suffering. Along with all the others who do not understand — or worse, who are implicated in the ordeal — God becomes the enemy who inflicts the pain on the hapless sufferer. Expressing anger, shame, and guilt over sickness, some victims raise questions that imply divine retribution: "Why did this happen to me? Am I being punished? Is God trying to say something to me?"[9] These hard questions pose a formidable challenge to the Christian caregiver. They also offer great opportunities to develop an activist theodicy.

Effective caregiving to those who are feeling vulnerable and abandoned is a delicate matter. One key to helpful assistance is to practice empathy and avoid exploitation. There is perhaps nothing more dysfunctional to caregiving than an attitude and approach that perceives the sufferer as an object to be manipulated for the caregiver's needs. This can occur whenever the caregiver enhances his or her own situation by imposing judgments on the sufferer, uses the sufferer's plight for selfish advantage, or simply unloads his or her own agenda on the suffering person. If the agenda is a religious one, sufferers are especially quick to realize that they are being abused rather than helped.[10]

The method of administering care to the lonely and unhappy is to empathize with them and share their suffering. Caregivers are to show by their actions that the sufferer does not stand alone in his or her plight. Empathy means to "feel into" another person's experience, "to sit beside another in his or her situation." Empathetic caregiving feels into the experience of the sufferer, sits beside him or her in his or her suffering. It is a mark of compassion to create "a sense of our common humanity, the realization that 'we are all in this together.'" Genuine caregiving is the result of being willing "to open ourselves to share another's burdens . . . to move from our secure and comfortable 'normalcy' or 'maturity' into the maelstrom of anxieties, doubts, pain, terror, and loneliness of the sick person's world."[11]

This empathetic relationship of the caregiver and sufferer is the doorway to recovery from the sense of isolation and guilt that plagues the sufferer. Genuine caregiving evolves from and produces a mutuality of perception that is healing both to the caregiver and the receiver of care. The caregiver sees her or his own sufferings in the person in need. Indeed, good caregiving will arise from helpers keenly aware of their own fragility and mortality. John Maes writes, "It is against the tapestry of our own pain that we understand the suffering of others. When we sit with the dying we have a sense of the territory because we recognize that we are looking at our own future."[12] Caregivers who are able to see their own suffering in the suffering of the other are likely to be more sensitive and successful in rendering assistance.

There is a "mirror dynamic" in good empathetic caregiving that helps those who suffer overcome their feelings of abandonment and victimization. First, the caregivers see themselves in the misfortune of the sufferer. They recognize past trials in their own lives and the prospect of illness to come similar to that of the sufferer. The caregivers see themselves in the situation of the sufferer.[13] At the same time, those who suffer see something of themselves in the caregiver. Good caregivers will convey their identification with the sufferer either by nonverbal language and gestures or by explicit narrative. Those who suffer will understand that the caregiver has been through similar crises in his or her life and is aware of the possibility of more to come. They will see in the caregiver a mirror of their own suffering. This insight establishes a covenant that enhances the credibility of the caregiver.

In the case of sufferers who are burdened by loneliness and guilt, caregiving can provide companionship and acceptance that overcomes those hurtful feelings. One of the vital actions in combating evil is that of sympathetic presence.[14] Sympathetic presence that arises out of empathetic identification expresses "unconditional positive regard" for the sufferer,[15] so that the sufferer comes to know and feel that he or she is no longer alone nor singled out for punishing judgment. This awareness that "trouble comes to all in various forms and at various times" can help those who suffer deal with their negative feelings.[16] The presence of an empathetic caregiver eliminates those unhelpful misunderstandings and restores balance in the sufferer's perception of what is going on in his or her own situation.

The beginning of helpful caregiving ministry is just at this point of companionship with the sufferer. As John Maes has said, "Patient listening and acceptance, the ability simply to 'be with' the sufferer, lies at the core of the helping relationship."[17] This being with and listening to the suffering person makes an important statement of several points. It says to those who suffer:

1. We identify with your plight.
2. We empathize with your trials.
3. We understand your misery.
4. We support you in your suffering.
5. We accept you, regardless of your situation.

This statement of acceptance and empathy can be the basis for significant spiritual growth in those who suffer,[18] and it is to that second level of the statement caregiving makes that we now turn.

Modeling the Divine Intent

Acceptance and empathy are two of the many important humane values in caregiving that can lead the sufferer to a deepening of faith. As Arthur Becker has said, we help those who suffer in order to strengthen their faith that God cares for them.[19] Caregiving that can address the intellectual problem of evil is that which is able to say something about *God's* relationship to that evil. The empathetic care that religious caregivers provide is an action of many ingredients, including the action of "symbolically modeling"[20] the divine intent and effort to "be with" the sufferer in his or her circumstances. Sympathetic caregiving says not only that we are present with, accept, and embrace the sufferer, but also that God is present with, accepts, and embraces the sufferer.

There is a helpful account of how this can work in a story by JoAnn Watson, a hospital chaplain assigned to a high-risk obstetrics floor. Upon short notice she married a couple in which the woman was soon to deliver a child. The joy of that event was shattered when, two days later, the boy died, another mysterious case of crib death. Chaplain Watson was stunned and depressed, but continued to provide what pastoral care she could. About a month later, Watson realized that her ministry had not been in vain, but had placed her as a companion with that new family in their ordeal. She writes,

> The healing of the pain of despair began when I realized that the tragedy did not diminish the good wrought by my care and concern. I was with Shandra and Noche in their suffering, and they felt my presence. That was all I could do. And yet that was enough. My ministry was not futile. The suffering, no matter how great, could not nullify or undo what I had done. I was a co-sufferer with them, and this was enough.[21]

Watson goes on to describe how this experience confirmed the significance of the cross for her, in a way similar to Jurgen Moltmann's concept of the Crucified God. She writes that her own suffering and despair allowed her "to fully realize that God has taken our suffering upon himself through the suffering of his Son on the cross and that he is capable of co-suffering with us . . . . Therefore when I suffer I know I do not go it alone."[22]

The realization that Watson came to is the heart of caregiving that overcomes feelings of being abandoned or judged by God. We hope that those grieving parents could see in their chaplain the presence of God in their suffering. Like her, they "did not go it alone," but were sheltered under the outstretched arms of the crucified God. When Christian caregiving makes that divine presence felt in the very midst of pain and loss, it sends a strong signal that those who suffer are not being punished by God or evicted from God's presence. It says God does not send the suffering but shoulders it with the afflicted and the caregiver.

Caregiving administered in the name of God or with Christian intent is never merely one person ministering to the wounds of another. In such compassionate care, there is the promise of a third party adding a divine blessing to the action. Kenneth Haugk assures the Christian caregiver,

> The presence and wisdom of God expresses itself through you as you relate to and care for others. . . . Jesus Christ is present in you as you care for others and in those for whom you care. . . . [Your] caring provides a channel through which God's love can flow. [Your] words and actions of love concretely demonstrate the good news.[23]

Human caregiving that conveys the presence of God works to overcome the awful loneliness and despair in suffering. The Christian caregiver must never underestimate the healing and strength that can occur when compassionate caregiving is all that it can be. As Marion Kanaly has said, "I come to offer a caring presence, an assurance of acceptance, a reminder of the divine presence and acceptance of the one who is for both the patient and myself Creator, Redeemer, Sustainer, the Ultimate Source of all that we are in our shared humanity."[24]

Empathetic caregiving says to the sufferer, "I am with you and God is with you." It says to suffering people that they are not alone, abandoned, victimized. All that negative baggage about "Why me?" or "Why is God punishing me?" is removed from the sickroom. In the compassionate and Christian care of the helper, the sufferer comes to see a companion and a divine presence. That supportive care clears the mind of the sufferer of all the clutter that the problem of evil dumps there. In the action of standing with the sufferer, the intellectual problem of evil fades away. The powerful witness of love "contradicts the abandonment the . . . patient may feel. If you, a finite, erring human being, are concerned enough to do away with the distance between you and the patient, how much more can a just and loving God?"[25]

CHAPTER TWELVE

The Alleviation of Suffering

In the previous chapter we explored how caregiving addresses the problem of God's role in evil and suffering as the caregiver mediates God's presence to the sufferer. That compassionate help says that God does not send suffering, but bears it with the sufferer and caregiver. We will now look at a second way caregiving speaks to the intellectual problem of evil. Insofar as the companionship of the caregiver also serves to relieve suffering, it declares that God is with the sufferer to help the sufferer overcome her or his pain or distress.

Does Evil Have the Last Word?

A second cluster of questions that often arises in the face of intense suffering includes, "Can my suffering be the meaning of life?" "Is evil the rule rather than the exception?" "Can I hope that goodness will win out over evil in the long run?" If the first question had to do with God's presence, this second set is concerned with God's power. In times of disaster, failure, pain, and suffering, it seems as though evil has gotten the upper hand. Empathetic caregiving may even heighten the feeling that suffering is the norm of life. To the degree that such caregiving is successful, and the caregiver truly identifies with the sufferer, it may seem that suffering has only multiplied, since the helper bears its burden as well. If the caregiver acts with religious intention, conveying God's presence to the sufferer, it might seem that suffering has even claimed God. Truly empathetic caregiving may cause the suffering person only to wonder if life is worse rather than better, since suffering is so widespread, afflicting sufferer, caregiver, and even God. In these circumstances, can there be any hope in God to resolve the issue, or is God just another victim like the suffering person?

This despair may seem to be only an extreme response to suffering, but it is not. A middle-aged man contracted a respiratory illness that limited his activity and hastened his retirement. Formerly vigorous and very active, this man was reduced to sitting in a chair for long periods of time and walking at a greatly reduced pace. He sold his farm, got rid of his horses, and gave up his dog-walking duties to his wife. Although the illness was not life threatening, it sapped the energy and vigor from this once robust outdoorsman. When I visited him, it was apparent he was suffering from a mild depression. Repeatedly, his lament was, "What next?" The issue for him was the future, and the future looked bleak and barren. He had lost all hope that life could be good again. For him only a dark cloud of defeat lay ahead. All life had been stolen from him, and evil ruled the day.

Daniel Foster notes that there are three types of questions that sufferers ask: informational, behavioral, and religious. The religious questions "have to do with meaning and destiny." They concern issues of fairness, the meaning of life, and both secular and religious hope.[1] I believe my suffering friend was asking a question about hope when he queried, "What next?" He was asking, Is there any more hope for relief? Will my condition worsen? What can I look forward to? I believe he was even probing the ultimate issue, namely, failing recovery, is there a hope in life after death? Underlying all these questions is the more fundamental issue of the ultimate goodness of life. When a sufferer asks about the future and what to expect, he or she is asking about the basic order of reality. Will it turn out good or evil? The sufferer perceives that evil has the upper hand now and wonders if it always will. There is a profound sense of despair that things may never get any better because everything is engulfed in the clutches of evil.

Oftentimes suffering prefigures death.[2] Even in mild illnesses, those who suffer are reminded of their finitude. The body is not immune from breakdown. It can be attacked by countless viruses, infections, and the ravages of aging. Surgery and the experience of anesthesia remind sufferers that death can strike at any moment. Just the physical experience of "going under" anesthesia, losing the awareness of one's mind, facing the black darkness of medically induced unconsciousness, can arouse premonitions of death.[3] The experience of anesthesia seems similar to what we have come to expect death to be like. The loss of consciousness and feeling is so abrupt and complete, unlike anything in life, including falling to sleep, that the sufferer wonders, Is this what death is like? All these sickroom experiences turn the mind to questions of mortality and threaten the soul with feelings of hopelessness. They raise doubts about the power of God to prevail. Will suffering be the sad song of the universe, or will God's sovereignty somehow conquer all?

Love Has the Last Word

In the previous chapter we noted how just *being* with a person is an *action* that brings human companionship and conveys God's presence to the sufferer. Standing alongside the sufferer to help shoulder his or her burden is an active response to suffering that says the sufferer is neither alone nor a victim of divine retribution. While that is a vital ingredient in an activist approach to suffering, it is not the whole answer. So long as suffering persists, another level of action is needed: namely, action to reduce the amount of suffering so far as is possible.

Earlier we discussed the response to evil that focuses on God's companionable suffering in the world. While that is an important part of religious devotion, it provides little help in solving the problem of suffering. While being with people in their distress is some help, it is not a sufficient response. In fact, there is something basically wrongheaded about proposing companionable suffering as the answer to the problem of evil in order somehow to assist the suffering person. The act of sharing suffering is performed in order to help the sufferer cope. That is to say, it is caregiving intended to alleviate at least the mental, emotional, and spiritual anguish of the sufferer. So compassionate companionship in suffering is not an end in itself, but a means to some other end, namely, the relief of suffering. It is therefore not enough to suggest that all we can do or should do is "be with" the sufferer.

The value in suffering with others is precisely in the fact that it is an action that brings some *relief* from suffering. The sufferer is comforted in her or his distress merely by the compassionate presence of the caregiver. This may not be made explicit in the strategy, but it is true, nevertheless. Now, what is implicit in that companionship is made explicit in active effort to alleviate suffering. Action directed to lowering pain, assisting recovery, or increasing comfort for the sufferer is an overt expression of what is covert in empathetic presence. To lend help to the sufferer in overcoming his or her distress is to express the intent of sympathetic companionship. It is to make explicit what is implicit in that empathy.

The kinds of caregiving that speak to the problem of evil are as numerous as there are people in need of care. John L. Maes writes about the roles of the caregiving team: "This more active side of caregiving includes a wide range of responses including medical and surgical procedures, nursing care, feeding and cleaning, education, priestly activities, and communications (with family, friends, businesses, etc.)."[4] All these professional and official forms of caregiving, when overlaid with religious meaning, are statements about the problem of evil.

Effective action against suffering will deal with the whole person and her or his unique needs. Those who take such action should be aware of Abraham Maslow's hierarchy of needs—physiological, safety, belongingness and love, esteem, self-actualization—and administer care accordingly.[5] The following example of caregiving for an automobile accident victim includes several levels of response:

> I got out of my car and crossed the road. The injured man was an older gentleman, wearing a suit. A slight trickle of blood ran from his mouth and when his eyes met mine, they seemed to plead: "Help me." I knelt down, unsure of what to do. He was obviously in pain. I quietly introduced myself and noticed that the trooper's jacket the old man was using as a pillow had slipped out from under his head. As I repositioned his head on the jacket, he mentioned his name was John.
>
> The old man's eyes brimmed with tears as he told me what had happened. I listened. After talking for a while, he said, "You're very kind."

> I quietly thanked him and smiled. No other words were necessary.
> After a few moments he added, "I'm scared."
> I grasped his hand and said, "I'll stay here with you."
> The twilight had faded and night was approaching. John began to
> have some trouble breathing. "Could you loosen my tie?" he gasped.
> "Of course. I'm sorry. I should have done that before."
> As I loosened his tie and unbuttoned his top button, a small silver
> crucifix slipped out.
> "You wear a cross. You're a Christian?" I said.
> John smiled a painful smile and replied, "Yes, I am."
> "Me too," I said, smiling back.
> After exchanging a few more words about the faith we shared, I
> asked him if he would like for me to pray with him. He answered
> affirmatively. We talked for a few moments about what he wanted to
> include in the prayer. Many of his concerns were obvious. All I had to
> do was look around. There were some key items, however, that I was
> glad he made specific mention of, because I would not have included
> them otherwise. We prayed. God's love seemed to envelop us both.
> As I was sharing with John my favorite verses from Psalm 139, the
> sound of an ambulance grew in the distance. Simultaneously, a car
> pulled up behind mine and a man and woman ran over to us. It was
> John's sister and brother-in-law. As they left together in the ambu-
> lance, I prayed: "Lord, go with them."[6]

In this account we see action that includes (in order) medical,
emotional, physical, spiritual, and familial caregiving. Each one of
those acts of assistance makes a statement to the problem of evil.

The caregiver must never underestimate the importance of basic
services as actions with significant import. Fitzhugh Mullan records
this tender story of caregiving from a veteran nurse assigned to
offer him care:

> Once when I was feeling particularly wretched she gave me a bed
> bath. When she finished it, she insisted that I spend ten minutes with
> my feet in a tub of warm water. I demurred at first, but she persisted
> and I gave in. When I was done, she patted my feet dry and put me
> back in bed. The relaxation and intimacy of the foot bath left me
> feeling mellow, pampered, and peaceful in a way that I had not
> known in many weeks.[7]

That personal care was a healing balm on the psyche of that over-
stressed patient. Had it been connected to any religious roots it
surely would have soothed his soul as well.

One case of ministering to basic needs that seems to have helped a
sufferer come to terms with her spiritual anguish is that of Carol

Schuller. Struggling with the loss of her leg in a tragic motorcycle accident, Schuller documents her spiritual journey in a frank and revealing remembrance. There were many times of deep depression and spiritual emptiness as she tried to make some sense of her misfortune. In the end, however, she emerged with a strong faith in God's care and help.[8] Part of the reason for the survival of her faith was the good caregiving she received from others (this reader counted forty-one helpers in her book): "Had it not been for my family and the priceless friends God had given me . . . I don't know what would have happened."[9] One of the key figures in that healing drama was her father. Interestingly, it was not only the spiritual help he provided that restored her faith, but also the care he gave for her physical being. So important was that basic care that she frequently writes of what would seem to be trivial events. She tells of a toe massage one day when forbidding pain racked every other part of her body. She records the day her father interceded on her behalf for pain medication. It was her father who asked about her sleeping and eating, and brought her favorite bath soap to the hospital. Dad was the engineer who rigged up a seat that enabled her to take her first shower.[10]

Caregiving that helps to alleviate suffering can come in a great variety of forms. It may take the form of teaching highly stressed patients relaxation therapy.[11] This may be combined with or replaced by assistance with exercises in meditation.[12] The caregiver may help the sufferer simply by reading to him or her or talking about events in the past and present. Doing something to alleviate suffering may take the form of telling one's own story of sickness to a suffering person who is desperate for information and assurance.[13] The sharing of one's own suffering is a "theology of experience"[14] that can help the caregiver to handle his or her own distress, and in that assistance say something to the problem of evil. All the forms of active caregiving, from footwashing to storytelling, can have theological import. These activist responses are not bookish, systematic, or dogmatic theological answers, but answers "birthed in distress, shared in pain, and created in the reality of immediacy."[15]

Among the needs of suffering persons are spiritual needs. These needs should be addressed in any caregiving that is directed to the whole person. A well-rounded caregiver will be a spiritual care provider as well as one who helps look after more basic needs. In some cases suffering people will readily seek and accept spiritual caregiving. In others it may be important to provide space in which sufferers can sort out their spiritual feelings. In still others, a little help with uncovering spiritual depths may be needed. Kenneth Haugk outlines three steps that may "open the door for the expression of spiritual needs":

1. Provide an atmosphere of acceptance.
2. Be alert to spiritual needs.
3. Encourage people to discuss spiritual needs.

He also lists several pitfalls to avoid, including one-way discussions, religious cliches, and a know-it-all attitude.[16] We would also add that the caregiver should avoid arguing with the sufferer about theodicy issues, although this is implied in the precautions noted. These fairly simple guidelines can help caregivers provide effective spiritual support. In providing that support caregivers are saying by their actions (and possibly by words of faith as well) that they want to help alleviate the sufferer's distress, and that God wants to help alleviate that distress also.

It should not be overlooked that spiritual caregiving can also be an important factor in alleviating physical suffering. There is evidence that the use of prayer and meditation can be efficacious in the relief of pain, providing a "spiritual anesthesia" that can lower distress and discomfort.[17] These religious practices can reduce the amount of anesthesia or pain medication needed by the patient.[18] Prayer can be explicitly directed to that purpose, as when the caregiver and sufferer join in "prayerful thought about what can be done to redistribute or to avoid stresses."[19] The prayer may simply offer an annoying situation to God as a way to reduce stress. Or it may encourage the sufferer in the development and maintenance of stress-reducing activities. Or it may merely be directed to incorporating a sense of the presence and grace of God in the soul of the sufferer. Such a spiritual goal can have the side effect of refocusing the center of a person's attention away from pain and reinvesting that energy in an intentional fellowship with God. It can turn a person's "helplessness into a conscious comradeship with God."[20] Those spiritual accomplishments can unleash healing attitudes and energies into the life of the sufferer, thereby contributing to the alleviation of suffering.[21] They are yet another way that caregiving as an *action* can make a statement about human and divine compassion.

All the kinds of caregiving we have noted, from foot-bathing to prayer, are actions that combat despair and restore hope. They challenge the feeling that evil is sovereign in the world. In place of that pessimism, caregiving action encourages the sufferer to believe that love, not evil, is the last word. This is the promise: "As a distinctly Christian caregiver, you can become a facilitator of God's hope. . . Your consistent, caring presence with them through thick and thin instills hope."[22]

Caregiving that conveys the love of people and God to the sufferer throws an altogether new light on suffering. It introduces the healing power of compassion into the discord of evil. When the caregiver empathetically takes on the pain of the sufferer, and conveys God's empathetic support as well, love overshadows that pain. Self-sacrificing care that also echoes the self-giving God of Christianity is a declaration of love that is unsurpassed. There is no greater love than that of the caregiver who relinquishes security and comfort to become vulnerable to the pain and distress of the afflicted. In such extraordinary moments evil is bested by a compassion that does not count the cost, but is concerned only to see misery overcome.

Empathetic caregiving can transform a grim and desperate situation into one of positive value and ennobling vision. Self-giving caregiving can transform the present suffering through a process that Margaret Spufford describes as

> somehow absorbing darkness—of physical or mental suffering of one's own, or worse of someone else's—into my own person, my own body or my own emotions. We have to allow ourselves to be open to pain. Yet all the while we must resist any temptation of assenting to it being other than evil. If we are enabled to do this, to act as it were as blotting-paper for pain, without handing it on in the form of bitterness or resentment or of hurt to others—then somehow, in some miracle of grace I do not begin to comprehend, some at least of this darkness may be turned to light.[23]

The power of love to overcome evil is a moment of grace in which the sufferer can see that evil is not triumphant, but love is.

It is possible that the worst that suffering can do to us can be subsumed beneath the best that compassionate care can do for us. Good can have greater lasting power than evil. Love can outshine the awful valley of the shadow of suffering. While Fitzhugh Mullan experienced anxiety, depression, and hopelessness in his bout with cancer, he also experienced a great outpouring of caregiving. Although not given to theological interpretations, he did discover the superior strength of love over evil in the care he received. And more than the bad he endured, it is the good that forms the residue of his experience: "What I remember and cherish are the people who commiserated with me, helped me, rooted for me, pinch-hit for me, and eventually cheered for me."[24] Could there be a better testimony to the power of compassion to overwhelm the power of evil?

Long-suffering love is a personal triumph in which one person helps another regain a sense of the goodness of life. In the love of the caregiver, the sufferer sees that there is a force in the universe stronger than evil, and that that force is love. Human caregiving can also underscore the fact that God's love is the final principle of reality. Acts of mercy in alleviating suffering are penultimate statements of the ultimate victory of God's goodness. Evil does not have the last word either now or finally. The care of one human being for another, when administered with Christian intent, says that the all-embracing rule of reality belongs to God, who acts for the healing of creation. As companionable care announces that human love can overcome evil in particular instances, so, when offered in the name of God, it says that God's love triumphs over evil in the grand order of things.

Caregivers who choose a ministry of service to sufferers reflect a God who chose a cross as the way to triumph over evil. Those who stand with victims in the name of God witness to the truth that God's love can reach into the seemingly most forsaken situations and redeem them. Such care says we must discern between what is reality and what is appearance. While it appears that evil is triumphant in life, the reality is that love is stronger than evil. The abiding truth that caregiving trumpets over the battlegrounds of life is that God's love is from everlasting to everlasting. It remains and abides to heal the wounded heart and restore the mind clouded by the problem of evil.

The Case of Intractable Suffering

What if the caregiving process is involved with an illness or crisis that is likely only to get worse? The suffering of those affected could still be considerably reduced through holistic caregiving. The action of alleviating suffering would still be possible and still make a statement about the problem of evil. But what about the illness itself? Suppose there is no hope that the basic source of the suffering can be overcome? Is there still any place for an activist theodicy, or is such an effort cancelled by the negative prognosis?

Stephen Schmidt describes three such cases of intractable suffering: Steve suffers from Gardner's syndrome, a progressive disease that creates growths and tumors in the body; Karen has multiple sclerosis (MS), a chronic progressive disease that causes the body to deteriorate; and Sophie suffers from diabetes, hypertension, and terminal cancer.[25] Presumably the prognoses in all these cases is very poor. Caregiving can do little to reverse the inevitable fatal outcome of those maladies. What then becomes of an approach that attacks the intellectual problem of evil by aggressive battle against and victory over suffering? Is there simply nothing to be said to Steve, Karen, and Sophie, since there is nothing that can be done to overcome their illnesses?

There are things that can be done to make the sufferer more comfortable, to reduce pain, and to maximize the quality of life that is left. But what can be done about the underlying reality of the situation, the fact that there is no way to overcome the relentless, destructive course of the illness? Of course, there is no escaping death, and "the denial of every form of suffering can result in a flight from reality."[26] But we are not speaking of a denial of death, but of disease, sickness, misery, and the premature end of life. It is reasonable to hope these evils can be overcome. However, what is to happen in cases where this does not seem to be likely?

There is still the need and possibility for action in the case of unrelenting suffering. If the conditions of suffering cannot be changed, at least the sufferer's perception of his or her suffering can be changed. Effective caregiving will help the sufferer reach a stage of acceptance that can, in turn, enable a positive management of the crisis. If reality will not yield to caregiving, if a cure or the relief of pain is not feasible, then caregiving action can focus on changing the sufferer's understanding of what is happening and the way it is handled. This is no less an action that overcomes evil, but it is tailored to the limits set by the circumstances given.

Caregiving may enable the sufferer to pass through several stages on the way to a successful management of the crisis. It may help the sufferer deal with the shock and insecurity that come with facing a terminal illness. It may aid the sufferer in working through and moving beyond stages of aggression and negotiation. It may provide companionship and support in depression, and it may have a strong impact on helping the sufferer reach a stage of acceptance and the resolve to make the best of the situation. Finally, caregiving can join caregivers with the patient in taking control of the remaining fragments and days of life, to distill the most meaning from them.[27] All these actions assist along the way toward a constructive coping with illness and crisis that would be useful in any situation of suffering, but are especially significant where the malady itself cannot be overcome. They provide the actions that make the most of a tragic situation, which is another way of saying they make the least of the anguish, despair, and resignation that threaten to engulf the sufferer.

Caregiving extended with Christian intent can help the chronically or terminally ill person confront her or his affliction with faith. A situation that may be hopeless so far as physical relief or a material cure are concerned may yet be changed by faith. Christian caregiving that instills faith in God can bring radical change into a hopeless situation. Kenneth Haugk lists the following benefits to the sufferer from distinctly Christian caregiving:

1. Stronger ties with a Christian community.
2. A better understanding of suffering.
3. Acceptance of forgiveness and grace from God and others.
4. An ability to forgive and love.
5. Increased trust.
6. Trust in the love of God.
7. A renewed experience of God's love and care.
8. Trust in Christ's continuing presence.
9. A Christ-centered stability.
10. A Christ-centered self-image.
11. Peace and wholeness.[28]

This list of benefits is really a description of what faith can mean in times of illness. They are profound attitudes and understandings that can revolutionize the way a person looks at life. In the case of those who can receive no more help for a fundamentally threatening condition, the impact of faith can be enormous. It can be the only positive ingredient in an otherwise dismal forecast. It may be the only meaningful expression of caregiving left for the caregiver.

These results or benefits of Christian caregiving are also a statement addressing the problem of evil. A suffering person who experiences those dimensions of faith is experiencing an "answer" that all merely rational theodicies miss. In the case where nothing else can be done to alleviate or stop the source of suffering, this statement is especially meaningful. A caregiving ministry that is able to strengthen such faith at the final point of life is not only the crown of a compassionate ministry, but the quintessential action of an activist theodicy.

In the cases of Steve, Karen, and Sophie, Christian faith was a vital part of their changed perception and the management of their illnesses. For Steve, faith meant a sense of purpose, hope, and overcoming the fear of dying. For Karen, faith meant a feeling of companionship ("I sometimes feel I have an angel with me") and a courage to accept the outcome of her disease. In the case of Sophie, Christian faith gave her confidence and an assurance that God loves and cares for her.[29] Each found relief in his or her faith. Their belief in God was the final cure, the ultimate therapy, the saving treatment that gave hope and triumph to their situation.

Faith worked for them to open up a closed future, to bring light to a darkened valley, to nurture a vision of better things to come. Any caregiving that is able to encourage or instill such faith is caregiving that makes a significant difference. There is action and there are results in such caregiving. Although the course of evil may be progressive, and it appears that it will win, the faith of the sufferer effectively changes the outcome. The end is not defeat, but a testimony to love. The sufferer has been held in the embrace of the caregiver and carried in the arms of God. Even where evil wreaks its worst, caregiving that builds faith gives love the final word and God the ultimate glory.

CHAPTER THIRTEEN

God's Gift of Autonomy

One can readily imagine that some people, on arriving in heaven, will march right up to God and ask, "Why did you choose the way that you did? Why did it take so much suffering to get here? Why this way and no other?" For these people it will not be enough that they have attained their everlasting reward, that at last they dwell in a land where pain is no more, neither crying nor discomfort. All that will be well and good, but it will not be enough of an explanation about God's role in suffering to lock in a satisfactory theodicy. For these troubled saints the question will still remain, Why was the road to paradise paved with the flames of hell?[1]

"Why Suffering in the First Place?"

The intellectual problem of evil is not one problem but a cluster of problems. We have already considered questions about abandonment and a lack of meaning. There is a third type of question that some sufferers raise as they wrestle with the problem of evil. This question comes from the deepest depths of suffering, and asks, "Even if evil is overcome in the long run, why is there any suffering at all?" This fundamental reality of evil will trouble many of us as

long as there is any suffering, as long as evil arises to claim children
and innocent sufferers. This question will be a problem, no matter
how effectively caregiving blunts suffering's harsh edge. The merest
incidence of gratuitous suffering shouts to heaven for justification,
muffling whatever statement caregiving makes on the problem.

This question is primarily about the ultimate goodness of God.
We have seen how the question "Why me?" focuses on the presence
of God. The question "Is there any hope?" raises issues dealing
largely with the power of God. This question about "Why any suffering at all?" has to do with the benevolence of God. To be sure, all
these dimensions of the problem arise in each question, but some
dimensions figure more prominently in certain questions than in
others. For example, while it is the presence of God that addresses
questions of isolation and feelings of victimization, it is God's presence as a loving God that is important.

The statement that caregiving makes on the question of whether
evil or good has the last word is a statement about which force has
the most power, which will be victorious, penultimately and ultimately. It is the triumph of caregiving love, human and divine, that
constitutes this statement. Since this question about the goodness
of God also raises the issue of the origin and necessity of evil, this
question is intertwined with the others about the power and presence of God considered above.

Nevertheless, it is primarily the goodness of God that is at stake
in this most profound level of the problem of evil. It is not enough,
these tortured sufferers feel, that suffering is being alleviated by
caregiving. A good God and a good world would not permit gratuitous evil in the first place. A good outcome can solve the problem
only if evil is somehow necessary to that good.[2] No amount of helpful action that reduces suffering, including divine action, helps with
the question of where evil comes from or why God allows it.[3]

While a religious approach to evil will try to defeat suffering, the
philosopher in us will attempt to understand how suffering can be
justified when it is overcome.[4] Actually, the tough-minded concern
for justification is part of our religious struggle with evil. For the
issue is, how can a good God allow evil to arise in the first place?
Once compassionate caregiving has made its statement, what can be
said about generic evil, the suffering that seems inherent, seems a
given, in the human situation? For all the help caregiving is, we still

have a problem on our hands. Can we show that suffering is an irreducible part of the human condition? What can we say to that problem by our activist approach?

Illness and the Loss of Integrity

The path through this thorny issue goes to the center of the experience of suffering and caregiving to ease suffering. There is one dimension of suffering that is especially relevant to this issue, namely, the experience of worthlessness and loss of control. Fitzhugh Mullan, a doctor, describes this experience when he writes about being wheeled to the recovery room clad only in a sheet:

> At one point during the wait I was awakened by an attendant who pointed out that the sheet had slipped and my numb behind was exposed. He asked me rather aseptically to cover it. His concern seemed to be about germs rather than sex, suggesting that I was more patient than person — an attitude I would come to know well.[5]

Dr. Mullan, who had declined premedication, "fearing perhaps any more loss of control," was acutely aware of the infantilizing impact of illness. He was a person accustomed to being in charge, and his hospital experience introduced him to an altogether new world of helplessness and dependence. His need to rely on others for assistance made him feel awkward and out of place: "I was a bad fit, a seven-sided peg in a hexagonal hole."[6]

Sickness can be a serious threat to a person's self-esteem. People who have been self-reliant and active are suddenly placed in a situation of acute dependency. This radical reversal of roles can trigger all sorts of insecurities and self-doubts. One observer put it this way: "Illness impairs one's productivity. It suggests idleness and weakness and dependency. Since self-esteem is related to self-reliance and independence, their loss can arouse shame or embarrassment."[7]

Sickness assaults the integrity and "intactness" of a person. This can be as true for the emotional, psychological, and spiritual self as for the physical self. As disease or disability attack the cohesion of the body, so they corrode the structure of the person's psyche as well. Activities through which the person expressed herself or himself — employment, family life, contacts with friends, recreation — are curtailed or lost altogether. Decisions, tasks, and accomplishments that effectively define the being of the person are withdrawn from the patient's domain of control and action. Much of the suffering of illness lodges just at this rupture of identity:

> When a person's self-image is assaulted by the losses of illness, emptiness results. Those whose identity has been molded by being active and productive may feel diminished, with nothing significant to contribute. . . . Depression is a common reaction to loss. The symptoms of depression include feelings of worthlessness, self-doubt, a lack of energy and an inability to concentrate.[8]

Perhaps the most painful and debilitating suffering is this bombardment against the core of the self. The loss of a limb, physical function, or years of life can contain a more primary loss, the loss of autonomy. The sick person is no longer able to do the very things that once defined his or her very being. The decline or abrupt ending of whole areas of deliberation and action is a surgical procedure far worse than any in the operating room, for the very center of the self is in danger. John Woodcock speaks of this in general terms: "Serious illness often involves threats to the patient's identity—unexpected and profound psychic, moral, and metaphysical challenges."[9] In particular, identity is a direct function of freedom and control. When those two qualities are compromised, the self is diminished. Without the ability to choose or manage our lives, we are only a shadow of ourselves. At its core, esteem rests in the capability of directing one's life, the responsible discharge of that privilege, and the comfort of knowing one did the best one could do.

Illness removes those ingredients of humanity from the life of the person. It attacks the integrity of the self by denying to him or her the rights of self-determination. It shatters the dignity of the person by creating limitations and dependencies. This is the very deepest depth of suffering, not to have the freedom to manage one's self-active structure, the autonomy to be all that one would choose to be. In that terrifying loss lies the greatest challenge to caregiving. Action alleviating that suffering also harbors a possible answer to the pesky question of why there is any evil in the first place.

Caregiving as Restoring Humanity

The Talmud contains a wonderful directive for wholesome caregiving. Out of respect for the indwelling Spirit of God who hovers over the bed of the sick one, visitors should not place themselves at a level above the patient. If the ill person is confined to bed, the visitor must not stand over the patient but sit on a chair or stool. If the patient is stretched on the ground, the visitor should respectfully sit on the ground. Wherever the ill person is, the visitor must not assume a superior posture so as to flaunt her or his own well-being and mobility. Rather, the visitor should respect the dignity of the sick person and the God who hovers nearby through an act of deference and humility.[10]

The important point in this lovely instruction is the emphasis on protecting the dignity of the sufferer. Interestingly, this is connected to respect for the Spirit of God. As we show respect for the person, we honor God. Our worship of God is bound up with our loving care of others. Of course, this is just the spiritual valence that makes caregiving so important to the dealing with the problem of evil. We will say more about that shortly. The primary focus of that story we want to point to now is the importance of affirming the worth of the sufferer. Effective caregiving will counter all those threats to self-esteem we have noted. It will restore the integrity of the patient and his or her sense of self-worth. Good caregiving not only should bring the caregiver to the level of the sufferer, it should also lift the sufferer to the level of the caregiver. That is, it should help the sufferer recover her or his identity, the capability to be an active self. It should return to the mind and hands of the sufferer the self-constituting deliberations and actions that illness has pirated away. In short, effective caregiving will help the sufferer regain freedom and control so far as is possible.

If sickness infantilizes the sufferer, caregiving should restore the rights of adulthood. It should facilitate the climb from dependency to autonomy. In broadest terms, it should aid in the move from disorganization (helplessness) to reorganization, where the patient decides how to make the best of his or her situation.[11] One of the most important goals of caregiving is to remove the sufferer from a state of helplessness so far as possible, and to relocate that person in a situation of self-management. So far as is possible, it should return to the sufferer's domain those areas of control that have been stolen away by illness. Effective caregiving will shift the status of the sufferer from victim to agent. The key in all this, of course, is a recovery of autonomy, the right to preside over one's own self-formation and destiny.

A story that shows how important a sense of self-worth is and how this is directly linked to freedom and control is the case of Mr. Moore, a middle-aged man in the terminal stages of malignant melanoma. Although terribly emaciated, this man complained little and showed no signs of giving up. Curious about his strength of spirit, several medical students arranged for an interview. During their visit, they learned that Mr. Moore was a painter. Eagerly, the sick man brought his paintings out for all to see. Several pictures depicted his battle against his disease. While showing his paintings and talking about them, an amazing thing happened: Mr. Moore seemed completely pain-free and showed no sign of his chronic nausea.[12]

What had kept this man going? In the interview he said, "Maybe I'm stubborn. All I know is, I'm not ready to die."[13] The experience in his room suggested far more reason than that. Clearly the activity of painting had given focus and purpose to his life. It was one area where he could exercise his freedom and creativity. Although he could control little else, he could paint what he wanted. From that creative activity he gained a sense of self-worth. All this reinforcement was dramatically illustrated during the interview, when his nagging symptoms disappeared. The recovery of his self-esteem through his painting revealed an oasis in his otherwise barren hospital stay. He received back from that creative activity and its product all the dignity stripped from him by his sickness. Yes, he may have been stubborn. But more than that, he had found an area where he was in control, where his own will and talents could be expressed. That recovery of his core self helped to keep him alive and to nurture his will to live.

Caregiving that reduces the helplessness and threats to self-esteem that sickness imposes can significantly alleviate human suffering. John Maes is right on target when he says, "When sufferers are treated seriously, as persons of intrinsic worth, healing can take place."[14] Restoring the sense of self-worth of a person is often a matter of restoring autonomy and control to that person. Caregiving that helps to do that lowers the level of suffering and thus is another aspect of caregiving that says something to the problem of evil, that the way to deal with suffering is to overcome it so far as possible. It says that even in terminal conditions, there is something that can be done. But more important, it responds to the question of this section: Even if evil is being overcome, why must it be there in the first place? Evil is there because the very autonomy that underlies our self-worth, esteem, and dignity can also create severe problems in our life.

This fact is clear when those who are sick do recover some autonomy and management in their lives. While in a dependent state, a patient has far fewer matters to decide or act upon. However, if autonomy is restored, the number of things for which a patient is responsible can increase rapidly. A sick person exercising self-management will face decisions about the kinds and level of care she or he will receive. With the power of self-determination at hand, the sufferer will need to deal with the future and all the issues it raises. As part of the recovery of identity, an afflicted person must decide how to relate to family, friends, and other helpers. All these arenas of autonomy raise the possibility of new problems for the patient. They increase the likelihood of new levels of suffering. As consciousness and control go up, the potential for more complex evil increases.[15] Keeping this whole scenario in mind—the problem of helplessness, the work of caregiving in restoring autonomy, and the new levels of suffering that can follow—let us move on to the final point.

God's Graciousness in Granting Autonomy

Caregiving that restores integrity, when administered with Christian intent, symbolically models God's action of creating and caring for human beings. Caregiving that addresses the intellectual problem of evil will point beyond itself to the role of God in the crisis. It will bring to the situation of suffering and helping theological content and "meaning-making."[16] The way that such caregiving can achieve this higher level of impact is by conveying the care of God in its action. Caregiving attains theological meaning by "caregivers, called to do the work of healing, who stand in the place of God."[17] When those who receive care understand that, then the help they receive is theologically meaningful. This understanding is never more crucial than when dealing with the question of why there is evil in the first place.

The story from the Talmud about visiting the sick is again significant at this point. As noted, the reason for a deferential posture is both to honor God and to show respect to the patient. But are not those two actions interrelated? Do we not honor God through our respect for the sick? Does not our worship of God include care of the needy? At its best, caregiving will be an act of devotion by the caregiver, and it will be received by the sufferer as a ministration from God. This dual focus is particularly important for the question of why we have evil, for in order for human caregiving to speak to that issue, it must be experienced as an analog of God's caregiving.

Caregiving addresses the question of why we have evil when the sufferer sees in that care an image of the God who cares. The way the caregiver helps is by affirming the worth of the person, in particular, by restoring autonomy and control. That caregiving is the human equivalent of a divine creativity and caring that respects human integrity by granting autonomy and control to human beings. The theological analog to suffering is nonautonomous human existence. Such an existence is a diminishment of human nature and life. To be without option, deliberation, judgment, choice, and capability is to suffer a less than completely human mode of being.

However, God, the ultimate caregiver, rescues us from that muted humanity by granting autonomy and self-management. As the center of human caregiving is a compassion that serves the sufferer, so the center of God's caregiving is a graciousness that affirms the creature. Effective caregiving will enlarge the being and world of the sufferer, suggesting the divine love that seeks only to enhance the life of the other. It will model that *agape* that intends and acts for the welfare of the world by giving it independence and self-management. God creates the world and human beings as somewhat removed, affirming their integrity as genuinely distinct self-governing parts of creation. The affirmation of human autonomy is the first inference that good caregiving can suggest.

The second insight is that the autonomy that makes us human also exposes us to suffering. A sick person who regains management will reenter the world of complex evil. To recover a sense of self-worth means a renewed struggle to protect and maximize that worth. As noted, the kinds and levels of suffering will rise as the sufferer returns to the complexity of life.

Similarly, the graciousness of God in granting us autonomy means that we become more vulnerable to suffering. Grasping that autonomy, we rise in dignity and worth, the capacity to think, feel, make judgments, and act intentionally. But we also enlarge our capacity to do harm and to feel more deeply the pains of life. It is not that evil will necessarily follow, but that it will likely follow. With the gift of autonomy, the situation changes. It is no longer the case that human beings can do no evil. And, in fact, what we see are traces of evil throughout human experience. Like the wind, we may not know whither evil comes or whither it goes, but the effects of evil are fairly obvious. With that precious gift of autonomy and self-management a new world is created, a world in which the possibility of suffering ever looms on the horizon.

Evaluation of Activist Theodicy

The activist approach to the problem of evil outlined in this chapter and the previous two avoids several of the pitfalls of theoretical theodicies. First, action addressed to the problem of evil does not fall into the trap of inflated language. This approach does not promise more than it can deliver. It is not made up of words that are empty, comforting platitudes that do not comfort. By its focus on action, it avoids these snares of rational theodicies. While an activist theodicy has a logic to it, it is not an argument. While there is a rationale to this approach, it is not a rational exercise. This strategy speaks by doing something, it is a declaration by deed, a statement made by standing up to and struggling against evil. In this approach, action speaks for itself, and the "medium is the message" in a most profound sense.

The action of caregiving is the heart of an activist theodicy. Human caregiving is a vehicle for divine caregiving. Superimposed over human action are suggestions of divine action on behalf of the sufferer. Compassionate caregiving delivered with Christian intent excites certain theological meanings. The sufferer sees God at work in that caregiving as a companion to, not a cause of, the suffering, as a helper who means to alleviate suffering, and as the Lord who gives worth and dignity to human beings. These are the meanings that address the questions that make up the intellectual problem of evil.

To be sure, an activist theodicy may include words that would likely be part of all stages or aspects of caregiving. They would be included in the companionship offered, the help in alleviating suffering, and the restoration of a sense of dignity and self-worth to the sufferer. Words may also help convey the Christian intent of caregiving through Scripture reading, prayer, and teaching. This would especially be true with the third set of questions concerning why we have evil, where the point is more complex than in the other two. But even there, verbal counsel would be given only as an illustration of action. The words would derive from the deeds, for the action is the primary thing to be said, the foremost message to be conveyed. The theological meanings that accompany the message are not argued, but are coaxed out of the action of the caregiver and the understanding of the receiver of care.

The reason an activist theodicy is not empty words that do not comfort is that such a theodicy rests on substantial action. Insofar as there is action to help the sufferer, an activist theodicy will never be a shallow or inflated answer. The action centering and driving such a theodicy is real and consequential, fundamentally credible and convincing. Like God's active word that does not return to God empty (Isa. 55:10-11), caregiving that goes out to sufferers is a statement that has content and consequence, and accomplishes that for which it was sent. No matter how dimly it may be perceived as addressing the problem, the action is irreducible. It is the center of the answer to the problem of evil, and so long as that caregiving occurs, it will be a response of substance to the problem.

Second, an activist theodicy does not compromise God's power or goodness. Unlike pessimistic theodicies that imply that God sends suffering to human beings, caregiving conveys the message that God abhors evil and intends that it be overcome. In the supportive companionship, help in alleviating suffering, and affirmation of the worth of the sufferer, caregiving aggressively affirms the divine opposition to evil and God's unqualified fight against it. It affirms in an activist mode the truth of Dorothee Soelle's statement that "the God who is the lover of life does not desire the suffering of people, not even as a pedagogical device, but instead their happiness."[18] Action to overcome suffering, delivered with Christian intent, avoids any tampering with God's goodness, but rather grounds and secures that goodness with a love-in-operation expression of discipleship.

Nor does an activist theodicy weaken the power of God. Unlike theodicies of hopelessness that totter on the premise of a limited

God, loving caregiving gives the sufferer every reason to hope that God will be effectively present to contain and diminish the suffering. Human caregiving that reduces suffering gives the sufferer confidence that God has the wherewithal to intervene, presently and ultimately. As the caregiver adopts the sufferer as a son or daughter, giving comfort and help as parent to child, so the sufferer feels the supporting arms of the heavenly Father and receives a foretaste of that final adoption as children of God in the everlasting kingdom. An activist theodicy imparts a vision of a world where the grip of evil is broken and the triumph of God is working itself out in the lives of all who are cast down in suffering and shadowed by death (1 Cor. 15:22-28).

Third, an activist theodicy does not turn the badness of suffering into good. There is no effort here to use evil or blunt its harsh edge by suggesting it is a megaphone to wake us up or instruct us. There is no energy wasted on trying to persuade sufferers that the world is better for their having suffered in it. An activist approach sees suffering for what it is: a sword, not a megaphone. It presumes that the better world is one where evil is absent or at least kept to a minimum. There is no room in an activist theodicy to negotiate with evil for good benefit. To the contrary, the strategy is to help the sufferer by reducing suffering. The center of the ministry of Jesus was directed to curing the sick, giving sight to the blind, and lifting the lame to walk. That is also the center of an activist theodicy. To deny that truth, to attempt instead to glorify suffering or make evil good, is nothing short of a Christian heresy.[19]

The activist method of overcoming suffering rather than negotiating with it is clear in the case of companionship and in helping to alleviate pain and distress. It is also relevant when dealing with the question of why there is any evil at all. In this third case, caregiving models God's gift of autonomy, and autonomy is the seed bed of complex evil. This more elaborate statement does not so much justify evil as suggest its source. The question of why there is evil is largely a question about the source of evil, not the justification of evil. If the suffering person has been guided through the earlier questions, then the issue is no longer one of justifying God. The sufferer understands that God does not send evil and does not use it for divine purposes. The sufferer also recognizes there is no point in appealing to the best-possible-world argument since an activist theodicy assumes that this world is far from the best but that it could be better through faithful caregiving. Therefore, God cannot be indicted on those counts and needs no defense. The issue why there is any evil, then, can be addressed by showing its source in the autonomy inherent in human integrity. That lesson in no way constitutes a rational theodicy that makes evil good, but is an insight that points to its origination in the human condition.

Conclusion

The sun rises when morning comes, the mist rises from the meadows, the dew rises from the clover; but, oh, when will my heart arise?

— Welsh, traditional

There is no problem more depressing for the human soul than the problem of suffering. Whatever its form, it casts a cloak of darkness that is all-encompassing. Suffering suffocates the spirit, deprives the mind of sense, and saps every drop of energy from the body. It is an endless night that forbids the dawn of meaning and hope.

In an attempt to dig out from under the oppressive weight of suffering, some people construct rational theodicies. The arguments in these theodicies, however, do not hold off the night, for they are propped up by a faulty theology.[1] They collapse when their notion of God as limited or uniquely good is uncovered, or when their denial of genuine evil is exposed. As their theology falters, their arguments fail, leaving nothing but rubble as a monument to the rational effort.

In response to the devastating senselessness of suffering, we have developed in this book a new approach called carevision that places caregiving at the forefront of a solution. We have outlined the biblical roots, theological components, and practical shape of caregiving. We have argued for a God-centered focus and an activist form for effective caregiving, and have shown how God's creative and redemptive support of the world is the driving force in an activist approach to the problem of evil. Thus, human caregiving is both written into the orders of creation and called for in Christian discipleship. As we surveyed the contemporary terrain—environmental, political, intellectual, and personal—we saw how caregiving can make an impact on the general landscape of life today.

In this book we have also considered how carevision relates to the problem of evil. Caregiving with Christian intent is an answer to the various questions that constitute the intellectual problem of evil with its accompanying fears and feelings of divine retribution, abandonment, and loss of self-management. Good caregiving addresses all those issues and implicitly says that God is not the cause of evil, but a companion in suffering. It also conveys the truths that God is with sufferers to reduce their distress, and that God's gift of autonomy explains why there is evil in the first place. These three statements are made to the problem of evil not in the mode of rational formulas, but by compassionate, helpful actions that symbolically model God's caregiving role in the suffering. Together with the action of caregiving, these statements constitute the response to evil called carevision.

Carevision is the strategy of choice for believers. The weight of suffering is especially burdensome for those who believe in God. Howard Burkle has correctly said that believers have to suffer not only the pain everybody else endures but also the "anxiety of knowing that these very evils also count against their religious beliefs."[2] Believers suffer the pain of perplexity about God's implication in their suffering. This intellectual problem of God's role in suffering is a problem for which God is uniquely responsible. If it were not for belief in God, the problem would not arise. If one simply gave up belief in God, then the problem would also go away.

However, to give up faith in God is to surrender the only hope for a response to evil that can stand and endure. The highest irony in the problem of evil is that the faith that creates the problem is the very faith that comes under attack by the problem. But the solution is not to give up the faith, but to turn it to use in solving the problem. This is done when believers find in the Christian message and call to discipleship the activist option in response to evil. The very faith that complicates suffering is the resource for overcoming the problem. Those who are most heavily stressed by suffering are also best located for dealing with that stress. Believers need look no further than their own heritage and commitment to find an answer to the problem of evil. In this sense, Christianity is especially well positioned to engage the issue. It is the very nature and mission of the Christian life to be the body of Christ in the world for its healing and redemption.[3] The solution to the intellectual problem of evil is hidden in that call. By living out that faith and servanthood, believers embody the unique strategy of Christianity for handling the problem of suffering.

Therefore, we must work ever more diligently to develop the activist part of carevision. Nevertheless, the selection of the caregiving option is not automatic for all believers. Although it is inherent in the Christian religion, the option of doing something about suffering is not always visible to the believer. Habits of thinking obscure its value for formulating a theodicy. In order for the Christian fellowship to be all it can be in servanthood and in a sane response to evil, several harmful perspectives have to be changed.

For one, defeatism needs to be overcome. This is the habit of ending the Christian story at the cross rather than the resurrection. Defeatism places the climax and sum of Jesus' life at the crucifixion. In this thinking, the cross is the perfect expression of Jesus' obedience and the fullest model for the life of discipleship. On the cross, God and the world are reconciled through the sufficient human sacrifice of a contrite spirit. While this thinking may represent a *part* of the Christian tradition, it is only a part and will result in a partial approach to the problem of evil. It locks on to the wrong target with the wrong weaponry: it focuses on the suffering itself, before which it displays the cross. In contrast, a *full* Christian response will center on the overcoming of suffering and the message of the resurrection.[4]

A second attitude that hinders favoring the caregiving option is religious masochism. This is the belief that suffering is *needed* because of guilt.[5] One of the frequent responses to sickness is a feeling of responsibility for the suffering endured. The sufferer feels the burden has been "visited upon" her or him because of past or present transgressions. Some sufferers grasp their suffering as the penance required by the moment. They believe they need the pain as a crucible where their lives can be refined and made pure again. This attitude, however, is neither Christian nor wholesome. If the activist option is to receive a fair hearing, masochism needs to be replaced with a gracious gospel and a healthy dislike for pain. The sufferer needs to hear that pain is not God's will, and guilt is not the Christian way. The gospel is the end of all punishment and the beginning of all remedies to bring relief to human suffering.

A third attitude that must be discarded if caregiving is to be a viable option is negativism. This is the point of view that says that to want relief from suffering is bad faith. This is the attitude that maintains that people who want God to intervene in a miraculous way to help them are guilty of abandoning Good Friday, of trying to take Christ off the cross.[6] Feeding on defeatism, this attitude goes one step further and insists that the proper religious response to suffering is to embrace it. Not only is the cross the model, but the way of suffering is the way of faithfulness. In this view, to want to overcome suffering is a case of deficient faith. Faith calls us to trust without knowing and to suffer without complaining. But surely all this is wrongheaded. While hoping for a miracle may be the sign of an overly ambitious faith, the negation of hope for relief of whatever kind is the sign of a perverse faith. We are no more faithful for stifling our instincts for relief and our trust that God can help. Rather, it is a lackluster faith that gives too little credit to the power of God and human caregiving. The religious story must lift our vision and strengthen our hands in caregiving, or what is faith for?

A fourth attitude that can weaken the impact of the caregiving option is futurism. This is the belief that nothing can be done to help the human condition now, but all will be rectified in a future kingdom or heaven. This otherworldly perspective is especially pervasive in times of suffering, when life in the world is hard. While it finds a good basis in Christian doctrine, it can unnecessarily devastate a program for the relief of suffering in the world. Futurism can also undermine itself if it is *only* otherworldly. Any credible hope in the future must be grounded in the present, as Teilhard de Chardin has said, "The expectation of heaven cannot remain alive unless it is incarnate. What body shall we give to ours today? That of a huge and *totally human* hope."[7] For the sake of heaven and earth, we need a "totally human hope" that things can be better in concrete ways in the real world now. Such a shift away from futuristic dreams to present realities is the very stuff of which an activist program is made.

All these negative sentiments must give way when carevision is cultivated. Carevision is the insight that it is by effective ministry to sufferers that we deal with the problem of evil. It is the outlook that turns to active caregiving as the strategy for dealing with that problem in times of suffering. What we need to know is that God does not abandon us to defeat but provides a way to overcome suffering. Carevision understands that God is with us to help us, but only as we are with one another in caregiving ministry. Carevision is an activist strategy to alleviate suffering. Carevision trusts the word of Scripture that in all perils and distresses, "We are more than conquerors through him who loved us," and that such victory is possible because nothing "will be able to separate us from the love of God in Christ Jesus our Lord" (Rom. 8:37,39). The bridge that connects that victory and grace to us in the real world now is human caregiving. We triumph in God's glory insofar as we help each other triumph in the battles of life. This is the *care* and the *vision* in carevision that conquers the darkness of evil and bids the shadows of doubt and despair flee away.

Endnotes

Chapter 1

1. Harry A. Cole, *Helpmates: Support in Times of Critical Illness* (Louisville: Westminster/John Knox, 1991), 135.

2. Christy Brown, *My Left Foot* (New York: Simon and Schuster, 1955), 80.

3. Daniel W. Foster, "Religion and Medicine: The Physician's Perspective," in *Health/Medicine and the Faith Traditions: An Inquiry into Religion and Medicine*, ed. Martin E. Marty and Kenneth L. Vaux (Philadelphia: Fortress, 1982), 255.

4. Scott D. Wright, Clara C. Pratt, and Vicki L. Schmall, "Spiritual Support for Caregivers of Dementia Patients," in *Journal of Religion and Health* 124 (Spring 1985): 35.

5. Fitzhugh Mullan, *Vital Signs: A Young Doctor's Struggle With Cancer* (New York: Farrar, Straus, Giroux, 1975), 43.

6. Richard F. Vieth, *Holy Power, Human Pain* (Bloomington: Meyer Stone, 1988); Stephen A. Wold, *Is God Still Here? The Comfort of the Cross for Those who Suffer* (Minneapolis: Augsburg, 1989).

7. Harold S. Kushner, *When Bad Things Happen to Good People* (New York: Avon, 1981).

Chapter 2

1. Kushner, *When Bad Things Happen.*

2. Herbert V. Prochnow, *Speaker's Handbook of Epigrams and Witticisms* (New York: Harper and Brothers, 1955), 121.

3. Elie Wiesel, *The Trial of God (as it was held on February 25, 1649 in Shamgorod): A Play in Three Acts* (New York: Random House, 1979). The chilling, unredeeming ending of this play cancels all hope in the goodness of God.

4. Emil Brunner, *The Christian Doctrine of God in Dogmatics*, 3 vols. trans. Olive Wyon (Philadelphia: Westminster, 1950-1979) 1:166-67; Patterson Brown, "Religious Morality," *Mind* 72 (April 1963): 236-44, and "God and the Good," *Religious Studies* 2 (April 1967): 269-76; John P. Reeder, Jr., "Patterson Brown on God's Will as the Criterion of Morality," *Religious Studies* 5 (December 1969): 235-42; Bruce R. Reichenbach, "Why is God Good?" *Journal of Religion* 60 (January 1980): 61-66.

5. C. S. Lewis, *The Problem of Pain* (New York: Macmillan, 1962).

6. Daniel J. Simundson, *The Message of Job: A Theological Commentary* (Minneapolis: Augsburg, 1986), 18.

7. *The Babylonian Talmud* (London: Soncino, 1936), vol. 3, chap. 4, Nedarim, 41a.

Chapter 3

1. Kushner, *When Bad Things Happen*, 120.

2. Kosuke Koyama, *Waterbuffalo Theology* (Maryknoll, N.Y.: SCM, Orbis, 1974), 73-76.

3. M. C. D'Arcy, S. J. *The Pain of This World and the Providence of God* (London: Longmans, Green and Co., 1935), 13, 15, 51, 71, 132.

4. Cyril E. M. Joad, *God and Evil* (London: Faber and Faber Limited, 1942), 66, 70, 108-12, 358-59.

5. J. S. Whale, *The Christian Answer to the Problem of Evil* (New York: Abingdon, 1936), 13, 51, esp. 54ff., 70-72.

6. Nels S. Ferré, *Evil and the Christian Faith* (New York: Harper and Brothers, 1947), 2, 18, 22-25, 68, 130-31.

7. Edwin Lewis, *The Creator and the Adversary* (New York: Abingdon, Cokesbury, 1948), 24, 40-42, 131-38, 154, 164, 170, 243.

8. Austin Farrer, *Love Almighty and Ills Unlimited: An Essay on Providence and Evil* (New York: Doubleday, 1961), 14-18, 49-50, 116, 123-24, 130, 151.

9. George Arthur Buttrick, *God, Pain, and Evil* (Nashville: Abingdon, 1966), 7, 8, 105-108, 125-30, 153-55, 224, 229.

10. Dorothee Soelle, *Suffering*, trans. Everett R. Kalin (Philadelphia: Fortress, 1975), 2-5, 130-37.

11. John K. Roth, *A Consuming Fire: Encounters with Elie Wiesel and the Holocaust* (Atlanta: John Knox, 1979), 85, 105, 155.

12. Kenneth Surin, *Theology and the Problem of Evil* (Oxford: Basil Blackwell, 1986), 130. See also pages 61-64, 134-35.

13. Wendy Farley, *Tragic Vision and Divine Compassion: A Contemporary Theodicy* (Louisville: Westminster/John Knox, 1990), 69, 87, 97, 111.

14. Dennis E. Saylor, *"And You Visited Me"* (Medford, Ore.: Morse Press, 1979), 22..

15. John B. Cobb, Jr., "The Problem of Evil and the Task of Ministry," in *Encountering Evil: Live Options in Theodicy*, ed. Stephen T. Davis (Atlanta: John Knox, 1981), 167.

Chapter 4

1. Haig Khatchadourian, "God Happiness and Evil," *Religious Studies* 2/1 (October 1966): 117.

2. W. Sibley Towner, *How God Deals With Evil* (Philadelphia: Westminster, 1976).

3. B. W. Anderson, "Creation," in *The Interpreter's Dictionary of the Bible*, 5 vols. (New York: Abingdon, 1962) 1:728, 730; Farrer, *Love Almighty*, 130.

4. Jon D. Levenson, *Creation and the Persistence of Evil: The Jewish Drama of Divine Omnipotence* (San Francisco: Harper and Row, 1988), 149-53. See also A. van de Beek, *Why? On Suffering, Guilt, and God* trans. John Vriend (Grand Rapids: Eerdmans, 1990), 331.

5. Daniel J. Simundson, *Where is God in My Suffering? Biblical Responses to Seven Searching Questions* (Minneapolis: Augsburg, 1983), chap. 2. See also Samuel E. Karff, "Ministry in Judaism: Reflections on Suffering and Caring," in *A Biblical Basis for Ministry*, ed. Earl E. Shelp and Ronald Sunderland (Philadelphia: Westminster, 1981), 95-97. Dorothee Soelle says it is bad advice to "learn to suffer without complaining." See her *Suffering*, 126 and 74.

6. John Hick, "God, Evil, and Mystery," *Religious Studies* 3/2 (April 1968): 546; Stephen A. Schmidt, *Living With Chronic Illness: The Challenge of Adjustment* (Minneapolis: Augsburg, 1989), 34-36; Surin, *Problem of Evil*, 52-53; Margaret Spufford, "The Reality of Suffering and the Love of God," *Theology* 88 (November 1985): 443.

7. Roland Puccetti, "The Loving God—Some Observations on John Hick's 'Evil and the God of Love,' " *Religious Studies* 2/2 (April 1967): 265; Edward Madden and Peter Hare, *Evil and the Concept of God*

(Springfield: Charles C. Thomas, 1968), chap. 2; Frederick Sontag, "Anthropodicy and the Return of God," in *Encountering Evil*, ed. Davis, 149.

8. Jurgen Moltmann, *The Crucified God: The Cross of Christ as the Foundation and Criticism of Christian Theology* (New York: Harper and Row, 1974); Terence E. Fretheim, *The Suffering God: An Old Testament Perspective* (Philadelphia: Fortress, 1984); Warren McWilliams, *The Passion of God: Divine Suffering in Contemporary Protestant Thought* (Macon: Mercer University Press, 1985). See also Howard Burkle's study of suffering in *God, Suffering, and Belief* (Nashville: Abingdon, 1977), 119-21.

9. Wold, *Is God Still Here?*, 61; see also p. 85. Galen Tinder, "Luther's Theology of Christian Suffering and its Implications for Pastoral Care," *Dialog* 25/2 (Spring 1986): 108-13.

10. Roth, *Consuming Fire*, 86. Not only is there little comfort, but it leads Roth to this very perplexing statement. How can he state the second part of his conditional, if the first part is true?

11. It seems that Stephen Wold (*Is God Still Here?*, 60) has possibly missed this dimension in citing Elie Wiesel's illustration in his novel, *Night*. Wiesel tells of the execution of a child during which someone in the crowd cried out, "Where is God now?" Wiesel says a voice within him said, "He is hanging here on this gallows." *Night* (New York: Hill and Wang, 1960), 71. From the context it appears that for Wiesel this was the death of God, a tragic symbol of God's ineffectiveness to help suffering humanity. See Graham B. Walker, Jr., *Elie Wiesel: A Challenge to Theology* (Jefferson, N.C.: McFarland and Co., 1988), 6-7.

12. John K. Roth, "A Theodicy of Protest," in *Encountering Evil*, ed. Davis, 17, 19, 61. Indeed, a merely suffering God is quite unlike the God of the Bible whom early Christians prayed to for help. See Sharyn Echols Dowd, *Prayer, Power and the Problem of Suffering: Mark 11:22-25 in the Context of Markan Theology* (Atlanta: Scholars Press, 1988), 88. This God is also unlike the God of faith whom believers have been taught "cares about us and has the power to help us" (Simundson, *Where is God*, 51).

13. Ronald Goetz, "The Suffering God: The Rise of a New Orthodoxy," *The Christian Century* (April 16, 1986): 388-89.

14. Alister E. McGrath, *The Mystery of the Cross* (Grand Rapids: Zondervan, 1988), 32-33, 41, 106, 188-89. But see also p. 176, and Gerald O'Collins, S.J. *The Resurrection of Jesus Christ* (Valley Forge, Pa: Judson, 1973), 129.

15. James McLeman, *Resurrection Then and Now* (Philadelphia: J. B. Lippincott, 1967), 243.

16. Walter Kunneth, *The Theology of the Resurrection* (St. Louis: Concordia, 1965), 18, 294-95.

Chapter 5

1. Gary Larson, *The Far Side: Gallery 2* (Kansas City: Andrews and Mc-Meel, 1986), 152.

2. Albion Roy King, *The Problem of Evil: Christian Concepts and the Book of Job* (New York: Ronald, 1952), chap. 4; Jeffrey Burton Russell, *The Prince of Darkness: Radical Evil and the Power of Good in History* (Ithica: Cornell University Press, 1988), chap. 3.

3. Fyodor Dostoevsky, *The Brothers Karamazov* (New York: Modern Library, n.d.), 261-68.

4. Gustaf Aulén, *Christus Victor: An Historical Study of the Three Main Types of the Idea of the Atonement,* trans. A. G. Hebert (New York: Macmillan Paperback, 1969), 47-80, 103-10.

5. Martin Luther, "A Mighty Fortress is Our God," Hymn 228, *Lutheran Book of Worship* (Minneapolis: Augsburg; Philadelphia: Board of Publication, Lutheran Church in America, 1978).

6. Rudolf Bultmann, *Kerygma and Myth: A Theological Debate* (New York: Harper and Row, 1961), 4.

7. Ben Johnson, "The Church, the University, and Biblical Belief," *Dialog* 26/1 (Winter 1987): 25.

8. Vieth, *Holy Power, Human Pain,* chap. 4.

9. See also Austin Farrer's *Love Almighty and Ills Unlimited*, 126, where he insists that evil is the result of *human* responsibility.

10. Vieth, *Holy Power, Human Pain,* 63, 80, 83, 85.

11. William Temple, *Nature, Man, and God* (London: Macmillan, 1934), 503-504; Whale, *Christian Answer*, 27; Buttrick, *God, Pain, and Evil*, 61-66; John Hick, *Evil and the God of Love* (New York: Harper and Row, 1966), 19.

Chapter 6

1. Morton T. Kelsey, *Healing and Christianity in Ancient Thought and Modern Times* (New York: Harper and Row, 1973), 54.

2. Frederick Houk Borsch, *Power in Weakness: New Hearing for Gospel Stories of Healing and Discipleship* (Philadelphia: Fortress, 1983), ix.

3. Edythe M. Daehling, *Ministries of Healing* (Philadelphia: Parish Life Press, 1984), 5.

4. Lewis, *Problem of Pain*, 10.

5. See Borsch, *Power in Weakness*, 67-84.

6. Saylor, *"And You Visited Me"*, 15-16.

7. Ibid., 12-15. See also Thomas A. Droege, "The Religious Roots of Wholistic Health Care: A Pastoral Response," in *Theological Roots of*

Wholistic Health Care, ed. Granger Westberg (Hinsdale, Ill.: Wholistic Health Center, 1979), 22. Droege notes that evidence of disease existing on the planet long before man's appearance "undermines any facile argument of theology that disease has its origin in man himself and can be explained solely in terms of human sinfulness."

8. Wold, *Is God Still Here?*, 12-13.

9. Joni Eareckson and Steve Estes, *A Step Further* (Grand Rapids: Zondervan, 1978), 18.

10. Vieth, *Holy Power, Human Pain*, 20-22.

11. Eareckson, *A Step Further*, 138.

12. Towner, *How God Deals with Evil*; Brain Hebblethwaite, *Evil, Suffering, and Religion* (New York: Hawthorn Books, 1976), 48; Francois Petit, *The Problem of Evil* (New York: Hawthorn Books, 1959), chap. 4.

13. Eareckson, *A Step Further*, 63-64.

14. Ibid., 55.

15. Joe Stevenson, "I Saw the Hand of God Move," *Guideposts* (February 1983): 20-23.

16. Philip Yancey, *Where is God When it Hurts?* (Grand Rapids: Zondervan, 1977), 107.

17. Eareckson, *A Step Further*, 117-21, 138-39, 144.

18. Yancey, *Where is God When it Hurts?*, 121, 148, 172.

19. David Hume, "Of Miracles," in *An Enquiry Concerning Human Understanding and Other Essays*, Essay 10 (New York: Washington Square, 1963), 108-128.

20. Joseph Fichter, *Religion and Pain: The Spiritual Dimensions of Health Care* (New York: Crossroad, 1981), 92-93.

21. Alexis Carrel, *Journey to Lourdes* (London: Hamish Hamilton, 1950), 41, 50-52. See also Theodore Mangiapan, "The Problem of the Lourdes Miracles," in *Lumen Vitae: International Review of Religious Education* 42/1 (1987): 19-33.

22. C. S. Lewis, *Miracles: A Preliminary Study* (New York: Macmillan, 1960).

Chapter 7

1. Eric Marshall and Stuart Hample, *Children's Letters to God* (New York: Simon & Schuster, 1966).

2. Hans Küng, *Eternal Life? Life After Death as a Medical, Philosophical, and Theological Problem*, trans. Edward Quinn (New York: Doubleday, 1984), 197.

3. Melvin Maddocks, review of Richard Marius's book, *Thomas More*, in *Time* (Dec. 24, 1984): 70.

4. Steve Martin, "Theologian of the Year," *The Wittenburg Door* 46 (Dec. 1978-Jan. 1979), 7.

5. C. S. Lewis, *A Grief Observed* (New York: Seabury, 1961), 23.

6. Eareckson, *A Step Further*, 73, 182-84.

7. Ferré, *Evil and the Christian Faith*, 105-206. See also Buttrick, *God, Pain, and Evil*, 153.

8. William Fitch, *God and Evil: Studies in the Mystery of Suffering and Pain* (Grand Rapids: Eerdmans, 1967), 123.

9. Hick, *Evil and the God of Love*, 399-400.

10. Hebblethwaite, *Evil, Suffering, and Religion*, 103.

11. J. Christiaan Beker, "Suffering and Triumph in Paul's Letter to the Romans," *Horizons in Biblical Theology: An International Dialogue* (December 1985): 105-19.

12. John Hick, "Appendix, Part IX. Immortality," in *Classical and Contemporary Readings in the Philosophy of Religion*, ed. John Hick, (Englewood Cliffs, N. J.: Prentice-Hall, 1964), 480.

13. Karl Barth, *Dogmatics in Outline*, trans. G. T. Thomson (London: SCM, 1955), 117.

14. See also Carl E. Braaten, *Principles of Lutheran Theology* (Philadelphia: Fortress, 1983), 83, 100.

15. For important discussions of this and other points, see Terence Penelhum, "Life After Death," in *Contemporary Philosophy of Religion*, ed. Steven M. Cahn and David Shatz (New York: Oxford University Press, 1982), 182-98; and Thomas McPherson, *The Philosophy of Religion* (London: D. Van Nostrand Co., 1965), chap. 10, esp. 148-52, 159.

16. Teilhard de Chardin, *The Divine Milieu* (New York: Harper and Row, 1968), 88-89.

17. Martin Luther, "Two Funeral Sermons, 1532," in *Luther's Works*, 55 vols., ed. Helmut T. Lehman and Jaroslav Pelikan (Philadelphia: Fortress, and St. Louis: Concordia, 1955-76), 51:251-52.

18. See Peter van Inwagen, "The Possibility of Resurrection," *The International Journal for Philosophy of Religion* 9/2 (1968): 121.

19. Frederick Sontag, "Critique" of Davis, in *Encountering Evil*, ed. Davis, 85.

20. John K. Roth, "Critique" of Davis, in *Encountering Evil*, ed. Davis, 89-91.

21. Soelle, *Suffering*, 149.

22. Frederick Sontag, "Anthropodicy and the Return of God," in *Encountering Evil*, ed. Davis, 57-58, 146.

23. On the way the meaning of the past can be changed by the future, see William Temple, *Mens Creatrix: An Essay* (London: Macmillan, 1949), and Hick, *Evil and the God of Love*, 399-400.

24. Stephen Davis, "Response" to critiques, in *Encountering Evil*, ed. Davis, 96. Interestingly, John Roth turns the tables and asks how Davis knows enough to say nothing can count *against* his hope (p. 91).

25. Roth, "Critique" of Davis, in *Encountering Evil*, ed. Davis, 89-92.

26. Beker, "Suffering and Triumph," 114.

Chapter 8

1. Roth, *A Consuming Fire*, 103.

2. Burkle, *God, Suffering, and Belief*, 98.

3. Xiao Yun, "The Teenager Who Gave His Life Fighting a Fire," *China Today* (June 1990): 11-12.

4. Nechama Tec, *When Light Pierced the Darkness: Christians' Rescue of Jews in Nazi-Occupied Poland* (New York: Oxford University Press, 1986), 165-166.

5. Arthur H. Becker, *The Compassionate Visitor: Resources for Ministering to People Who Are Ill* (Minneapolis: Augsburg, 1985), 11.

6. George W. Forell, *Faith Active in Love: An Investigation of the Principles Underlying Luther's Social Ethics* (Minneapolis: Augsburg, 1954), 122-23. Others would add economics, education, and sports as orders of creation.

7. Carl A. Volz, *Pastoral Life and Practice in the Early Church* (Minneapolis: Augsburg, 1990), 13-18, 20-21, 151-52.

8. Thomas Wilkens, "Ministry, Vocation and Ordination: Some Perspectives From Luther," *The Lutheran Quarterly* 29/1 (February 1977): 76.

9. John Bowker, *Problems of Suffering in Religions of the World* (Cambridge: Cambridge University Press, 1970), 116-18, 223, 265.

10. Joseph A. Bracken, S. J., *What Are They Saying About the Trinity?* (New York: Paulist, 1979), 49, 51, 81.

11. Forell, *Faith Active in Love*, 132-33; Donald C. Ziemke, *Love for the Neighbor in Luther's Theology: The Development of His Thought, 1512-1529* (Minneapolis: Augsburg, 1963), chap. 4; Ernst Troeltsch, *The Social Teaching of the Christian Churches*, 2 vols., trans. Olive Wyon (New York: Harper and Row, 1960) 2:528ff.; Philip S. Watson, *Let God Be God: An Interpretation of the Theology of Martin Luther* (Philadelphia: Muhlenberg, 1947), 110-16.

12. Koyama, *Waterbuffalo Theology*, 91-94.

13. Gustaf Wingren says vocation is the right care for office. See his *Luther on Vocation*, trans. Carl C. Rasmussen (Philadelphia: Muhlenberg, 1957), 115. Also see Donald R. Heiges, *The Christian's Calling* (Philadelphia: Muhlenberg, 1958), 46-48.

14. Keneth L. Vaux, "Theological Foundations of Medical Ethics" in *Health/Medicine and the Faith Traditions*, ed. Marty and Vaux, 209.

15. Emil Brunner writes that the Christian must search out ways for making the orders "more just, more humane, more full of the spirit of love." See his *The Divine Imperative* trans. Olive Wyon (Philadelphia: Westminster, 1947), 233.

16. Regin Prenter, *Luther's Theology of the Cross* (Philadelphia: Fortress, 1971), 11-14.

17. Ziemke, *Love for the Neighbor*, chap 2; Prenter, *Luther's Theology of the Cross*, 11.

18. Wingren, *Luther on Vocation*, 27.

19. William H. Lazareth, *Luther on the Christian Home: An Application of the Social Ethics of the Reformation* (Philadelphia: Muhlenberg, 1960), 113-14; Heinrich Bornkamm, *Luther's Doctrine of the Two Kingdoms in the Context of His Theology* trans. Karl H. Hertz (Philadelphia: Fortress, 1966), 22-24, 33-34; Paul Althaus, *The Ethics of Martin Luther*, trans. Robert C. Schultz (Philadelphia: Fortress, 1972), 66-78. It is in this sense only that pain could become a Christian's vocation, i.e., as a by-product of action to reduce the suffering of others. To make pain a vocation in the sense of a God-given order in life to be endured (Buttrick, *God, Pain and Evil*, chap. 12) is to overlook the whole biblical emphasis on God's battle against suffering. In view of that campaign the position of the Christian must be that our vocation is not pain but the alleviation of it. See Wayne E. Oates and Charles E. Oates, *People in Pain: Guidelines for Pastoral Care* (Philadelphia: Westminster, 1985), 133-34.

20. Gordon E. Jackson, *Pastoral Care and Process Theology* (Washington, D.C.: University Press of America, 1981), 237. Italics mine.

21. Wingren, *Luther on Vocation*, 129; Paul Althaus, *The Theology of Martin Luther*, trans. Robert C. Schultz (Philadelphia: Fortress, 1966), 34, 105-106, 118-19; John R. Loeschen, *Wrestling With Luther: An Introduction to the Study of His Thought* (St. Louis: Concordia, 1976), 150; Martin J. Heinecken, "Luther and the 'Orders of Creation' in Relation to a Doctrine of Work and Vocation," *Lutheran Church Quarterly* 4 (1952): 399.

Chapter 9

1. Rebecca S. Chopp, *The Praxis of Suffering: An Interpretation of Liberation and Political Theologies* (Maryknoll, N.Y.: Orbis, 1986), 3-4, 44, 151.

2. Buttrick, *God, Pain, and Evil*, 35.

3. Baron Friedrich von Heugel, *Essays and Addresses on the Philosophy of Religion*, second series (London: J. M. Dent and Sons Limited, 1926), 200.

4. Kelsey, *Healing and Christianity*, 90, 98.

5. Bowker, *Problems of Suffering*, 50, 54.

6. Richard Driscoll and Lloyd Edwards, "The Misconception of Christian Suffering," *Pastoral Psychology* 32/1 (Fall 1983): 38.

7. Riley B. Montgomery, *The Ministry of All Believers: The Pastoral Role of the Christian Ministry* (Lexington: The College of the Bible, 1962), 16.

8. Buttrick, *God, Pain and Evil*, 55, 105, 108.

9. Becker, *The Compassionate Visitor*, 26, 29. See also a Jewish rendering of the notion of reciprocity in Samuel E. Karff's essay, "Ministry in Judaism" in *A Biblical Basis for Ministry*, ed. Shelp and Sunderland, 90. Karff writes, "God's initiative toward the believer should be reflected in the believer's initiative toward others."

10. Borsch, *Power in Weakness*, 97.

11. Kenneth C. Haugk, *Christian Caregiving: A Way of Life* (Minneapolis: Augsburg, 1984), 34. See also p. 154.

12. Colin G. Kruse, *New Testament Models for Ministry: Jesus & Paul* (Nashville: Thomas Nelson, 1983), 190.

13. Ibid., 35.

14. Jens Glebe-Möller, *Jesus and Theology: Critique of a Tradition*, trans. Thor Hall (Minneapolis: Fortress, 1989), 33-37.

15. Heije Faber, *Pastoral Care in the Modern Hospital* trans. Hugo de Waal (Philadelphia: Westminster, 1977); Fichter, *Religion and Pain*; Thomas A. Droege, "A Brief History of the Relationship Between Religion and Medicine," in *Theological Roots of Wholistic Health Care*, ed. Westberg, 23-26; John N. Brittain, "Theological Foundations for Spiritual Care," *Journal of Religion and Health* 25/2 (Summer 1986): 107-109. Brittain writes, "While it has become traditional to speak of Hippocrates as the 'Father of Medicine,' in many ways it is the ministry to the sick of Jesus of Nazareth that has provided the model for the development of much of the Western tradition of health care."

16. Dorothee Soelle with Shirley A. Cloyes, *To Work and To Love: A Theology of Creation* (Philadelphia: Fortress, 1984), 41.

17. Wold, *Is God Still Here?*, 73.

Chapter 10

1. Bernard Martin, *The Healing Ministry in the Church* (Richmond: John Knox, 1960), 19-20, 23.

2. Morton T. Kelsey argues that, according to Scripture, salvation is one meaning of healing, not vice versa. Caregiving, therefore, is the more inclusive term, of which salvation is one form. See his *Healing and Christianity*, p. 109.

3. Becker, *The Compassionate Visitor*, 25.

4. Don S. Browning, "Mapping the Terrain of Pastoral Theology: Toward a Practical Theology of Care," *Pastoral Psychology* 36/1 (Fall 1987): 10-28.

5. Martin, *The Healing Ministry in the Church*, 31.

6. C. W. Brister, *Pastoral Care in the Church* (New York: Harper and Row, 1964), xxiii.

7. Morris Maddocks, *The Christian Healing Ministry* (London: SPCK, 1981), 60.

8. The inclusive base and expansive scope of caregiving is one reason an activist theodicy cannot be confined to or content with faith-healing as the major form of caregiving ministry in the church. While it may be a valid form of ministry, faith-healing tends to focus on the cure of health problems by religious leaders. In this regard, it subverts a ministry of the whole people of God to the whole spectrum of human suffering. For a description of faith-healing see, David Edwin Harrell, *All Things are Possible: The Healing and Charismatic Revivals in Modern America* (Bloomington: Indiana University Press, 1975).

9. Wesley Granberg-Michaelson, *Ecology and Life: Accepting our Environmental Responsibility* (Waco: Word, 1988), 21-23.

10. Ibid., 65-82.

11. Ibid., 157.

12. Ibid., 140.

13. Soelle, *Suffering*, 65-69.

14. Soelle, *To Work and To Love*, 55-57, 69-70, 98-101.

15. Soelle, *Suffering*, 2, 19-20, 142.

16. Ibid., 18, 125-126.

17. Ibid., 2, 5, 109.

18. Ibid., 72-73, 78. See also Vieth, *Holy Power, Human Pain*, 132-137.

19. Soelle, *Suffering*, 72-73, 149.

20. Soelle, *To Work and To Love*, chaps. 7, 8, 9.

21. Soelle, *Suffering*, 130-34.

22. Robert Ellwood, *The History and Future of Faith: Religion Past Present, and to Come* (New York: Crossroad, 1988), 23-24, 117, 118-21.

23. Douglas John Hall, *Thinking the Faith: Christian Theology in a North American Context* (Minneapolis: Augsburg Fortress, 1989), 48.

24. Ibid., 12-14, 57-65.

25. Ibid., 19, 30, 39, 75-80.

26. Erika Schuchardt, *Why is This Happening to Me? Guidance and Hope for Those Who Suffer*, trans. Karen Leube (Minneapolis: Augsburg, 1989), 19-21.

27. Ibid., 144-45.

28. Ibid., 128-29.

29. Ibid., 142.

30. Ibid., 137.

31. Ibid., 36-37.

Chapter 11

1. F. Pratt Green, "O Christ, the Healer, We Have Come," Hymn 360, *Lutheran Book of Worship*.

2. Fichter, *Religion and Pain*, 79.

3. Ibid., 29.

4. Oates and Oates, *People in Pain*, 125.

5. Robert Stromberg, "The Voices on Coronary Care: A Confrontation with Vulnerability," in *Hospital Ministry: The Role of the Chaplain*, ed. Lawrence E. Holst (New York: Crossroad, 1985), 132.

6. Marion Kanaly, "The Voices on a Surgical Unit: The Loss of Control," in *Hospital Ministry*, ed. Holst, 113.

7. Mullan, *Vital Signs*, 48.

8. Ibid., 43.

9. Stromberg, "Voices on Coronary Care," 131.

10. Mullan, *Vital Signs*, 54-55.

11. Becker, *The Compassionate Visitor*, 27-28, 38.

12. John L. Maes, *Suffering: A Caregiver's Guide* (Nashville: Abingdon, 1990), 147.

13. James A. Wharton, "Theology and Minstry in the Hebrew Scriptures," in *A Biblical Basis For Ministry*, ed. Shelp and Sunderland (Philadelphia: Westminster, 1981), 62.

14. Vieth, *Holy Power, Human Pain*, 110-114.

15. Haugk, *Christian Caregiving*, 81, 83-84.

16. Saylor, *"And You Visited Me"*, 17.

17. Maes, *Suffering*, 122.

18. Becker, *The Compassionate Visitor*, 51.

19. Ibid., 20.

20. Kanaly, "Voices on a Surgical Unit," 114.

21. JoAnn Ford Watson, "Reflections on Ministering in Suffering," *The Journal of Pastoral Care* 43/3 (Fall 1989): 278.

22. Ibid., 279.

23. Haugk, *Christian Caregiving*, 25, 26, 136.

24. Kanaly, "Voices on a Surgical Unit," 115.

25. Oates and Oates, *People in Pain*, 121-22.

Chapter 12

1. Foster, "Religion and Medicine" in *Health/Medicine*, ed. Marty and Vaux, 255-57.

2. Schmidt, *Living With Chronic Illness*, 118.

3. Mullan, *Vital Signs*, 17; Becker, *The Compassionate Visitor*, 21.

4. Maes, *Suffering*, 149.

5. Haugk, *Christian Caregiving*, 68-69.

6. Ibid., 129-30.

7. Mullan, *Vital Signs*, 126.

8. Carol Schuller, *In the Shadow of His Wings* (New York: Thomas Nelson, 1986), 215.

9. Ibid., 213.

10. Ibid., 19, 41, 43-44, 82.

11. Howard W. Stone, *Using Behavioral Methods in Pastoral Counseling* (Philadelphia: Fortress, 1980), 13-30.

12. Herbert Benson, *The Relaxation Response* (New York: Avon, 1975), 104-40.

13. Schmidt, *Living With Chronic Illness*, 83.

14. Ibid., 96.

15. Ibid.

16. Haugk, *Christian Caregiving*, 54-59.

17. Oates and Oates, *People In Pain*, 131-33.

18. Fichter, *Religion and Pain*, 92.

19. Oates and Oates, *People in Pain,* 126.

20. Ibid., 125.

21. Karff, "Ministry in Judaism," in *A Biblical Basis for Ministry*, ed. Shelp and Sunderland, 98.

22. Haugk, *Christian Caregiving*, 148-49.

23. Spufford, "The Reality of Suffering," 445.

24. Mullan, *Vital Signs*, 163.

25. Schmidt, *Living With Chronic Illness*, 101-11.

26. Dorothee Soelle, quoted in Schuchardt, *Why is This Happening to Me?*, 123.

27. Ibid., 28-37.

28. Haugk, *Christian Caregiving*, 143-46.

29. Schmidt, *Living with Chronic Illness*, 103-104, 107, 110.

Chapter 13

1. Frederick Sontag, "Critique" of Hick, in *Encountering Evil*, ed. Davis, 57-58.

2. Ferre, *Evil and the Christian Faith*, 13.

3. Buttrick, *God, Pain, and Evil*, 168.

4. William Temple, *Christus Veritas* (London: Macmillan, 1949), 256.

5. Mullan, *Vital Signs*, 15-16.

6. Ibid., 125.

7. Stromberg, "Voices on Coronary Care," in *Hospital Ministry*, ed. Holst, 131.

8. Ibid., 132.

9. John Woodcock, "Personal Experience of Illness: An Aid to the Practice of Medicine?" in *Perspectives from the Humanities*, The Milton S. Hershey Medical Center, 2/3 (November 1989): 2.

10. Karff, "Ministry in Judaism" in *A Biblical Basis for Ministry*, ed. Shelp and Sunderland, 90.

11. David E. Reiser and David H. Rosen, *Medicine as a Human Experience* (Rockville, Md.: Aspen Systems Corporation, 1984), 118-21.

12. Ibid., 146-51.

13. Ibid., 148.

14. Maes, *Suffering*, 64.

15. Paul Siwek, S.J., *The Philosophy of Evil* (New York: Ronald, 1951), 101.

16. Maes, *Suffering*, 23-24, 162-69.

17. Ibid., 170.

18. Soelle, *Suffering*, 108.

19. Spufford, "The Reality of Suffering," 444.

Conclusion

1. Surin, *Theology and the Problem of Evil*, 38.

2. Burkle, *God, Suffering and Belief*, 107.

3. Douglas John Hall, *God and Human Suffering: An Exercise in the Theology of the Cross* (Minneapolis: Augsburg, 1986), chap. 5.

4. Martin E. Marty, *Health and Medicine in the Lutheran Tradition: Being Well* (New York: Crossroad, 1983), 62-63.

5. Saylor, *"And You Visited Me"*, 19.

6. Schmidt, *Living With Chronic Illness*, 86.

7. de Chardin, *The Divine Milieu*, 153.